the between boyfriends book

the between

St. Martin's Press New York

boyfriends book*

You know that's when you'll read it, so now if you read it in public, men will know you're available

A Collection of
Cautiously Hopeful Essays
by Cindy Chupack

www.stmartins.com

The following stories appeared in somewhat differ-
ent form in *Glamour*: "Lone Rangered," "Sexual
Sorbet," "Relationship Equivalency Exam,"
"Halloweenies," "Your Number," "Relationship
Reruns," "Cupidity," "Last Call," "The Visa
Defense," "Male Friend Moratorium," "Snooze-
Lose Syndrome," "Sports Dates," "Dater's
Remorse," "Do Not Resuscitate Romance (DNRR)
Order," "The Frequent Crier Conundrum," "Close-
trophobia," "Retrodating," and "Premature
'We'jaculation." "The Rant" appeared in somewhat
different form in *Slate*, "Carmunication" in
Harper's Bazaar, "Going Hollywood" in *Allure*, and
"The *Real* New York Marathon" in *New York
Woman*.

Library of Congress Cataloging-in-Publication Data

Chupack, Cindy.
    The between boyfriends book : a collection of cautiously hopeful essays / Cindy Chupack.—1st ed.
      p. cm.
    ISBN 0-312-30903-1
    1. Single women—Psychology. 2. Dating (Social customs)—Humor. 3. Man-woman
relationships—Humor. 4. Separation (Psychology) I. Title.

HQ800.2.C48 2003
306.7—dc21

               2002045584

First Edition: August 2003

10   9   8   7   6   5   4   3   2   1

To my wonderfully funny friends
for their support between and during,
and to my parents and sister
for remaining cautiously hopeful

contents

more table of contents

it's not us . . . it's them

it's not us . . . it's the city

okay, maybe some of it's us

your new boyfriend

a brief note from the author

This collection is the result of many long, hard years of research, and by that, of course, I mean dating. I have written about dating and relationships for television (*Sex and the City*) and several magazines. The fact that I have lots of dating experience seems to be a plus to these people, even though I keep thinking that it should prove beyond a shadow of a doubt that I have no idea what the hell I'm doing.

One magazine recently offered me a dating advice column, and I said I would love to take that on if readers would be giving me advice, or if it could be a "bad advice" column in which I would offer helpful hints like, "Maybe your new boyfriend doesn't understand how much you love him. Call him more often! Surprise him at work! Bake him something heart-shaped! Cry after sex! Men can't get enough of that stuff."

I'd like to think the reason I've been successful writing about relationships (if not *in* actual relationships) is that I still believe in love, and I believe deep down all of us do. (Maybe not right after a breakup, but within the next calendar year.) I continue to date and write and hope, and hope to date Mr. Right. But given that I'm still single—or "between boyfriends" as I prefer to call it—and so many fabulous women I know are between boyfriends,

Author's Note

I'd like to say for the record that this book is not about giving advice. It's about commiserating and ultimately celebrating this crazy, heart wrenching, exhilarating time in our lives, because it doesn't last forever. It only seems like forever.

the breakup

chapter one

LONE RANGERED: To have had a relationship end in a mysterious and annoying way—with no good-bye, no answers, just the vague feeling that you have no idea who that man was.

Men are good at a lot of things. Breaking up is not one of them. When a woman wants to break up with a man, she invites him over for dinner, cooks his favorite dish, and tells him she's seeing his best friend. It's all very straightforward and diplomatic. But men have this weird aversion to endings. They prefer to take the passive mode, allowing the relationship to end itself. Men can't be bothered with dramatic farewells, the questioning of motives, discussions. They are bored. They want out. Good-bye.

I remember the first time a boy broke up with me. We were in the seventh grade. He invited me over after school, said he just wanted to be friends, then had his mother drive me home. It was all downhill from there. In more recent years, a doorman informed me that my date was not coming down. Ever. A friend called her boyfriend and found out he had moved to a new city. A coworker happened upon a personal ad placed by the man she was dating.

Every woman, with the possible exception of Cindy Crawford, has a story like this. She may have dated the man a few weeks or a few years. They may have shared a cab or an apartment. It doesn't matter. For some reason, the man thinks that the decision to break up is none of her business. (Of course, some women do the same thing. But then again, some women mud wrestle.)

Often a woman senses a breakup brewing and tries to get the man to sit down and fess up. This is futile. The average male gets this beam-me-up-Scotty look on his face as soon as you mention the word "discussion." He avoids subsequent contact as if you were trying to serve him a subpoena. Then, when you finally work up the nerve to ask him what the heck is going on, he pretends you're imagining the whole thing. It's all part of the game, and evidently the winner is the one who can quit the game without ever talking about it.

Some men admit they avoid confrontation because they're afraid we'll cry. Of course we'll cry; we cry at Hallmark commercials. What they don't understand is that we're not crying because of them, we're crying because now we have to get naked in front of someone else. It's enough already.

It's a rare and brave man who breaks up in person. Most likely he has sisters and does volunteer work. He'll say things you've heard before: "I'm unable to make a commitment. I don't have time to be the kind of boyfriend you deserve." Then he'll add, "I hope we can eventually be friends. I'd really miss your company." It doesn't matter if he's lying, telling the truth, or quoting something he read in a woman's magazine. At least he's trying.

Most men, however, think that even making a phone call to end a relationship is excessive. "What's the point?" they want to know. The humane thing, they've decided, is not to call, but instead to disappear like the Lone Ranger. These men believe in

"Close your eyes and make it go away." They believe in the Fifth Amendment. They believe in absentee ballots. They may ski black diamonds, walk barefoot on hot asphalt, skydive for fun, but measured on their fear of confrontation, these guys are wimps. They'll say they're going to the rest room and never return. Then they'll meet friends for drinks and say, "She just doesn't get it," or "What do I have to do, spell it out for her?" It's not that we don't get it. After about three weeks of shampooing with the water off—just in case he calls—we get the picture. But we'd like to feel like more than simply a notch in somebody's bedpost. Stranded without an explanation, we sound like the neighbors of a murderer. "He seemed nice. Kind of kept to himself. This came as a complete surprise." Underneath, of course, we know.

You can spot a woman whose relationship is disintegrating because her answering machine gives hourly updates of her whereabouts. "I'm at work now, but I'll be home by seven." "I'm at aerobics." "I'm in the shower." Meanwhile, *his* machine has the same message as always: "I'm not home. Later."

So what happens is this: you refuse to bow out gracefully, and he refuses to confront. His only option is to make you so miserable that you break up with him. We're talking emotional terrorism. It's fun, easy, and gets results.

During this period he won't laugh at your jokes. He'll ask you out, then act like you're imposing. He'll shred what's left of your confidence by saying, "You're wearing that?" He may even tell you he'd like to end the relationship, but continue sleeping with you. Then he'll act surprised when you bash in his headlights, stuff his favorite tie down the disposal, and ignite his baseball card collection.

So what's the right way for a man to break up? I suggest the following steps:

Step One: Choose a reason. Inevitably your girlfriend will ask why you're leaving, and you should be prepared to explain. If you know that your reason is petty and immature (I know a woman who broke up with a man because his nose looked like a penis), make up a nicer reason.

Step Two: Select a date that doesn't conflict with birthdays or major holidays. "I didn't plan to break up with her on Valentine's Day," a male friend once explained. "It just happened to coincide."

Step Three: Talk to her. You're both adults. It might go surprisingly smoothly.

Step Four: Hide your baseball cards.

chapter two

SEXUAL SORBET: The first person you sleep with after a breakup; a palate cleanser to remove the taste of a failed relationship.

Every time I go through a breakup (my average is approximately one every two years, although I'm trying to improve my time—get in and get out in under a year) I think my vast experience should make it easier. This is, of course, naïve, like expecting swimsuit shopping to get easier because you've been through it before. The reality is that breakups (like swimsuit shopping) get harder as we get older, maybe because we're not dating wildly inappropriate men . . . as often. Instead, we're dating men we genuinely thought could be The One, and when they turn out to be just the twenty-fifth, it's understandably depressing and annoying. To make matters worse, everybody has advice to dole out as you cry over your chicken Caesar salad: "These things take time. This is a loss. You're mourning the loss of the life you thought you'd have. You should go back to therapy or to that yoga class where they turn up the heat and people either feel amazing or pass out."

Well, I have advice also. I say sleep with someone else. Sexual sorbet cleanses the palate and prepares you for your next course. After all, you don't want your ex to be the last guy you slept with. You need to put some distance between the two of you, and five to seven inches ought to do it.

Now bear in mind I'm not talking about a rebound relationship. You're not ready for a relationship. This is strictly sex, and that fact should be communicated clearly to your choice of sorbet. My friend Kate sees the same guy every time she breaks up. She calls him "Interstitial Bob." (Although the last time she called Bob a woman answered the phone and Kate felt it was the end of an era.) I recommend old fling–flavored sorbet because that way you know what you're getting, plus it's a good use of those wildly inappropriate men who were great lovers but not much else.

Note: Men will most likely be wary and disbelieving when you tell them you're only interested in sex. They've fallen for that line before from women, and let's face it—casual sex is not our strong suit. But these are extraordinary circumstances and once you prove that your intentions are purely impure, you'll be surprised how many men are willing to rise to the occasion. Remember, every breakup is an opportunity to do it right the next time. And in the meantime, it's an opportunity to do it.

chapter three

"HEY BABY" WEIGHT: The weight you have to be at in order to date again and to have random men on the street call out, "*Hey Baby . . .*"

I am going on a ten-day fast. In preparation for this fast I have eaten most of the contents of my refrigerator, including leftover spare ribs (which I don't even particularly like) and the not insignificant remains of a small birthday cake. I now feel sick enough to abstain from eating for at least a day if not longer.

This fast is called the Master Cleanser, a.k.a. the Lemonade Diet because you drink six to twelve glasses of "lemonade" a day, the lemonade being a mixture of spring water, fresh organic lemon juice, maple syrup and a little cayenne pepper.

I believe this fast is medically sound because I know people who have done it. Well, okay, I know *one* person who has done it, but he knows other people who have done it and he himself does it every year for seven days. *And* there is a booklet. I realize that "booklet" does not sound very substantial. Most diets, however far-fetched, at least merit a book. But the Master Cleanser is written and advocated by a man who, when he is not fasting, survives on fruits, vegetables, seeds, and berries, so this is not a man who sends in a book to do a booklet's job, if you know what I mean.

The other thing I tell myself (and concerned others) is that this is Not About Weight Loss. I know I can't expect to keep off the pounds I shed while on a fast. I just want to cleanse my system and get rid of the toxins, plus I think after eating nothing for ten days, it will be easy to make smaller changes to my diet like eliminating those Magnolia Bakery cupcakes.

DAY #1

I have read the booklet so many times in preparation for this fast that by 10 A.M., I am already feeling most of the possible side effects, which are, of course, psychosomatic because I have yet to even make the lemonade. I prepare a big pitcher, while thinking that if I were going to pick a drink to live on for ten days, it would probably be something more along the lines of a banana daiquiri, but I suppose that would be considered a "problem" rather than a fast.

By late afternoon I'm a little hungry, and I notice the place where I really have a Pavlovian response is my kitchen. I make a mental note that *I'm not sure whether I go to the kitchen when I'm hungry, or whether being in the kitchen makes me hungry.* This is the kind of possibly profound thought you have when you are on a ten-day fast.

That night I go to see Nick Lowe at Joe's Pub in the Village, and I find that instead of watching him, I am watching the guy at a table in front of Nick Lowe, who has ordered a large bowl of penne and has only eaten half. He pushes the pasta to one side of the bowl and can't seem to finish it. I can't bear it. I don't understand why the waitress doesn't take it away so we can all go back to enjoying the concert.

DAY #2

You know how if you used to drink a lot at parties, and then you stop, you suddenly realize how stupid drunk people sound at parties? That's how I am about food today. I can't believe how many people say, "I'm starving!"

The truth is, we are not actually starving when we say we are starving. I know this because I'm not starving and I am essentially "starving." The downside of this new enlightened me is that I am right on the verge of becoming one of those women I hate—the ones who forget to eat and say food is not that important to them and begin their sentences with, "The truth is . . ."

I am reminded of an ex-roommate who had a big box of Neuhaus chocolates in her room that she must have received as a gift. She never ate one. And it was the assortment, so there had to be *something* in there that she liked. It became my ritual to beat her home from work, sneak into her room and check for missing chocolates, and as the days wore on and the chocolates remained I got increasingly upset at her restraint and/or disinterest. I knew we could never be friends if her psychotic eating disorder was going to continue. And now it seems I am her—for at least eight more days.

I did pass an important test tonight. I successfully had my first dinner out without having dinner. I had hot mint tea (which is sanctioned) while my friends/co-workers ate Italian. My profound thought for the evening was this: *Maybe conversation is like food. Maybe it can be just as satisfying.* But then the food came, and I remembered: *Conversation is not like food. Food is like food. Food is like an eggplant parmigiana.*

DAY #3

Okay, it's not about weight loss, but I have lost six pounds! I drink my lemonade proudly. I carry it in a water bottle knowing people will wonder what's in the bottle, happy to explain. I have plenty of energy. I am somehow getting through this. My only complaint is that despite how much time not having and planning and traveling to meals frees up, I am not being very productive. I spend the afternoon seeing a movie because that's two hours less I'll have to think about not eating, and then I discover my new favorite pastime—trying on clothes that didn't fit the day before.

DAY #4

I lost another pound! I must now figure out how to see the maximum number of people at this present and probably unsustainable weight. My friend Mark invites me to a Yankees game. Perfect. Yankee Stadium. Sold-out game. 56,000 people. Maybe I'll get on the Jumbotron.

By the second inning I realize that baseball games are not about baseball, they are about hot dogs, soft pretzels, peanuts, pizza, and beer. I didn't bring any of my lemonade, mainly because post–September 11th games have very tight security, and I didn't want to explain to some humorless guard that I had a special drink in my water bottle because I was fasting. I'm sure they know all about "special drinks," and Mark reminds me that fasting might be associated with Ramadan, which, in this political climate, is a red flag issue unto itself. So I reasoned that I would just drink water for the duration of the game, which was fine for the first nine innings, but by the *eighth* extra inning (Oakland A's, 8/9/02, look it up if you want) I was wondering, "What would one Cracker Jack do?" Mark bought a box and gave me his free prize. I thought: *Maybe prizes are like food. . . .* But this prize was not like food. It was just a stupid sticker. I was disappointed, almost depressed. I deeply wanted something three-dimensional, like a ring. Or a Cracker Jack.

DAY #5

I am not only surviving this fast, today I made it through a spin class. One happy thing is that I am not breaking out or having pains or cramps as warned by the booklet. At dinnertime I go out for sushi without having sushi, and sushi is my favorite. I am extremely impressed with myself. I also discover the recipe for frozen lemonade (blend with ice!), which almost approximates solid food and becomes the highlight of my existence.

DAY #6

I've lost nine pounds! I decide to hit another important benchmark—trying to entertain without food. This came about because last week I started a tradition of having friends over to watch the *Sex and the City* episode, and for that I put out a great spread, so this week I ask people to bring whatever they want, which for a notoriously over-the-top hostess is almost harder than not eating, and at 8:30 they show up and nobody has brought anything.

It is important to note that I am Jewish. Jews know it is not a social gathering without food. Jews feel downright uncomfortable with people in the house and no food displayed. Turns out my friends ate before coming in deference to my fast, but Mark, the same Mark who ate a whole box of Cracker Jacks in front of me at 1:30 in the morning at Yankee Stadium, did not eat first *or* bring anything, so he decides to order out for pizza. I generally haven't been too hungry, but his pizza looked awfully good. In any case, people didn't stay long after the episode. *Apparently the rest of the world still needs food in order to have a good time.*

DAY #7

Today, continuing on my path of seeing as many people as possible at this weight, I went to Madison Square Garden for the Bruce Springsteen concert. Not only did I make it through the concert (which was lousy with soft pretzels), plus a four-tiered tower of shellfish afterward at Balthazar, I made it through running into an ex-boyfriend over whom I've been known to exercise very bad judgment. The kicker: *I didn't sleep with him!* We went back to my place and we just . . . caught up. Profound discovery of the evening: *If I can sit in a restaurant with three desserts on the table and not eat, I can sit in my apartment with my ex and not have sex.*

DAY #8

I am down to my "Hey Baby" weight. I know this because I was walking down the street in a little skirt and blouse, and a construction worker looked me over and said, "Hey Baby . . ." *Apparently, for women there's baby weight and then there's "Hey Baby" weight.* The only side effect I'm suffering from is trouble getting to sleep. And I need sleep tonight, because tomorrow I am beaming my skinny self across the United States. Yes, it was an amazing coincidence of timing, but because of a trend I wrote about, I was asked to do an appearance on the *Early Show.*

DAY #9

The bad news: I only got four hours of sleep. That's the thing about the *Early Show*—it's very early. And you have to get up even earlier to look like you didn't just get up.

The good news: I have lost ten pounds! However, the camera adds ten pounds, so I figure I'm even. I was worried about doing the *Early Show* because a) I've never done live television, and b) it was scheduled for Day 9 of my fast, so in the sitcom version of my life, this is when my character would pass out, right there in the fake living room set while the cameras were rolling. My only consolation would be that very few people I know are up this early, and even fewer are watching CBS.

DAY #10

I have one scare in spin class when I finally get some genuine side effects. I have a gripping cramp in my stomach and a shooting pain in my shoulder. But I stay on the bike because the class just started, and the booklet implies that pain is a sign the fast is working, that bad toxins are being released. I hope that is what is happening, because the alternative is that I am going to die in spin class. I probably wouldn't be the first. As soon as we cool down, I feel fine.

So this is it. I have not eaten a bite of food in ten days. Forget winning an Emmy—this is by far the most impressive thing I have ever done. It's now All About the Weight. How to keep it off. How to keep my cheekbones. The booklet says you're supposed to stay on the diet for a minimum of ten days, but you can do it for up to forty. I briefly consider staying on the fast for forty days. Maybe someone could sponsor me. I could pretend to be doing it for a cause. This leads to my final profound thought: *As women, there are some things we can abstain from and some things we can't. Food, yes. Sex with an ex, yes. Obsessing about our weight, no.*

I finally decide not to continue the fast, because I did what I set out to do, and I am not Gandhi. I'm pretty sure Gandhi didn't jump on the scale every morning and shout, "Woo-hoo!"

Note to those who are tempted to try it: I managed to keep about half the weight off, but I must admit it was easier to be on the fast than it was to come off it, maybe because I tried to "adopt a diet of fruit, vegetables, seeds, and berries" as the author suggested. Suffice it to say that one night I actually left a note on my computer with directions on how to find this book. I eventually had to call my G-I doctor who said, "And why did you do this fast?" Then he suggested I have something bland like dry toast. I was about to tell him I was trying to avoid carbs, but I thought better of it and made the toast.

chapter four

RELATIONSHIP EQUIVALENCY EXAM: A test that would allow you to earn credit for past dating experience so you could pick up a new relationship where the old one left off.

There's nothing worse than almost marrying someone, breaking it off, and having to start over with a blind date. It's like failing your senior year of high school and having to go back to kindergarten. And now, thanks to the media blitz of all media blitzes, we know that single women don't have the time, patience, or eggs for that kind of setback.

I was happy to read that, despite all the hoopla (and there was significant hoopla, including the cover of *Time* magazine), Sylvia Ann Hewlett's book about the "epidemic of childlessness" is not selling. I love that it's not selling. I feel that by *not* buying this book (*Creating a Life: Professional Women and the Quest for Children*), thousands of fabulous, single, thirty-something, career-minded, childless-but-hopeful women like myself essentially covered our ears and said, "I can't hear you la la la."

The thing is, telling women—especially single women—that they need to hurry up and have children is like telling an elderly woman with a walker that she needs to get across the street faster. She *wants* to get across the street. She's *trying* to get across the street. Yelling that the light is changing and cars are coming will not help her get across the street.

One thing that *would* help us get across the street is shortening the time we spend in less-than-stellar relationships. And one reason these relationships can take years is that we've always had to start over from scratch. But no more, because I have devised the time- and egg-saving Relationship Equivalency Exam! The exam is completely unscientific, but until someone comes up with a better one, this is the standard. You and only you can determine whether your date's answer merits relationship credit, allowing him/her to place out of that particular relationship stage. This exam should be administered over drinks, because if all goes well, you might be moving in rather than going to dinner.

RELATIONSHIP EQUIVALENCY EXAM FOR MEN

1) English: What does it mean when you say, "I'll call you?"
2) Math: How many women can you have sex with and still be monogamous?
3) Psychology: Other than abject fear, what are some possible reactions to the words, "I love you?"
4) Economics: Who pays for dinner if your date makes more than you, and how long before you resent her for it?
5) Physics: Find a way to arrange your bathroom items on your half of the sink, knowing full well your girlfriend needs the whole sink for her items.

RELATIONSHIP EQUIVALENCY EXAM FOR WOMEN

1) English: When you say, "I'm not in a rush to get married," define the word "rush."

2) Math: Is the amount of minutes it takes you to evaluate a date as a potential husband more than or equal to the amount of minutes it takes you to identify and ignore the red flags?

3) Psychology: Other than abject fear, what are some possible reactions to the words, "I need space?"

4) Economics: How much should you pay for an apartment you never visit in order to keep a boyfriend from freaking out that you live in his?

5) Physics: Find a way to arrange your bathroom items on your half of the sink while still maintaining the illusion that you wake up looking this good.

Pencils down. Break up or marry accordingly.

the year ahead

chapter five

DATING HORRORSCOPES: Dismal astrological predictions to help manage the expectations of the newly back-on-the-market dater.

AQUARIUS: JANUARY 20—FEBRUARY 17

The planets are shifting in your favor, and you're in the power seat . . . for about a day. The Twenty-first. So don't sleep through it. The rest of the month you have no control over your love life whatsoever. You will fall for a string of men who just want to be friends, lose ten pounds, gain twelve, and contemplate lesbianism. Hang on though. By the end of the month, a relationship you have questions about will become even less clear.

PISCES: FEBRUARY 18—MARCH 19

This month is going to be a roller coaster, Pisces, so keep your hands in the car! You will meet an exciting new man on the Third, but find out he has a girlfriend. Another sexy stranger will come into your life on the Tenth (not as sexy as the first guy, but this one is at least available) and you will share an incredible night of passion, then he won't call you ever again. Sorry.

ARIES: MARCH 20—APRIL 19

Mercury (the planet of communication) turns retrograde the last two weeks of the month, so good luck to you! This is the perfect time to lay low. Read a book. Take up knitting. Any attempts at romance will end in disaster, but that doesn't stop you! Jupiter in Leo magnifies your parents' fear that you will never marry.

TAURUS: APRIL 20—MAY 20

Get ready! Your job is about to get much more demanding, especially near the full moon of the Twenty-first, which is good, because it will take your mind off the Breakup. Be aware that your superiors are under a lot of pressure, so they might be less tolerant of sobbing during work hours. Likewise, the phone sessions with your therapist might no longer be considered a valid reason to miss a meeting. Venus in Scorpio means all eyes are on you—so this is a good time to stop stealing office supplies. (Yes, Kleenex boxes are considered office supplies.)

GEMINI: MAY 21—JUNE 20

Take some risks this month. Although not risks like you took last month. You should *always* use a condom. But you know, some small risks, like asking out that guy you always see at the gym. He will turn out to be gay, but at least you put yourself out there. The Twenty-first is a good time to make changes, like switching to a different gym, or city.

CANCER: JUNE 21—JULY 22

This month your personal life is entering a happier chapter, but that's not saying much, because you have been a mess! The Thai delivery guy knows your order by heart. Your friends are starting to screen your calls. Your therapist checks her watch a little too frequently. Maybe it's time to stop wallowing in the past and look ahead to the future. Chin up! Once Venus is in Scorpio, Ben and Jerry's is coming out with a new flavor.

LEO: JULY 23–AUGUST 22

Travel brings new insights and sharpens your perspective. For example, you discover that in Guatemala you're considered a hottie. You will have a whirlwind romance with an international man of mystery, but since Mercury is in retrograde, the real mystery is . . . what the hell did you see in this guy? No time for questions—the full moon has Leos cohabitating. It's a miserable experience, but worth it when your ex hears Paolo's voice on your answering machine!

VIRGO: AUGUST 23–SEPTEMBER 22

Romance gets more complicated once Venus enters Scorpio on the Seventh, because after three months of sleeping together, you can no longer pretend you're just looking for "closure" with your ex. The planets are sorry to sound preachy, but closure is good-bye. Closure is a garage sale of his things. Closure is not late night booty calls spent rummaging through his bathroom for signs of another woman.

LIBRA: SEPTEMBER 23–OCTOBER 22

Your planets turn fickle this month. Pluto can't decide if you should live happily ever after or die alone. This thought might keep you up at night. You will be troubled by that whole "bird in the hand" thing and wonder if you should have stuck it out, but you did the right thing. Your ex was not The One. Or was he? End-of-the-month news of his engagement might set you back a bit.

SCORPIO: OCTOBER 23–NOVEMBER 21

Venus enters your sign on the Seventh, and you know what Venus rhymes with, so go find yourself one! It's time to have sex! Rebound city! You know, of course, that a rebound relationship can't go anywhere. But Mercury is in retrograde, so you will think you are madly in love, which will complicate things when the relationship crashes and burns around the Twenty-eighth.

SAGITTARIUS: NOVEMBER 22—DECEMBER 21

The new moon is the time to make decisions. Like where exactly *is* this "fling" with the twenty-two-year-old going? The planets are in conflict, especially the Seventh and Twenty-first, so that's not a good time to confront him about his pot problem. Mars in Virgo makes your health vulnerable, so camp out in Mexico at your own risk! An older boyfriend might spring for a hotel with a bathroom, that's all the planets are saying.

CAPRICORN: DECEMBER 22—JANUARY 19

The once-a-year new moon in your sign changes your course, so you'll try online dating, something you once contended was "for losers and psychos." Turns out you were right! You will spend much of the new moon trying to understand the point of being "open-minded," since you never imagined a coffee date could be so endless. You will tire of your own story and begin to make things up, which is dishonest but also helpful, because you will project a much healthier outlook on life thanks to your new childhood, family, job, and ex.

chapter six

THE RANT: A long, angry, and ideally humorous speech you will inevitably give or receive after one too many disappointing Valentine's Days.

Last weekend I confessed to a friend that I don't have a valentine this year. On cue, he launched into the Rant: The holiday makes more people unhappy than happy. It puts too much pressure on relationships by making romance mandatory, so even if you like doing something sweet and surprising for your loved one, it can't be surprising because it's expected. Why can't we each just pick our own Valentine's Day, he went on to ask. His could be, say, May Fifth—a day when he might actually get into his favorite restaurant.

I know the Rant. I've done the Rant. I had a fresh Rant last year when I was so busy I somehow forgot it was Valentine's Day until I wandered into a Duane Reade to buy detergent, and under the unflattering fluorescent lights, I came face to face with one of those white teddy bears holding a red foil heart balloon. I wasn't sure what was worse—the fact that the guy in front of me was buying the Duane Reade bear for his girlfriend, or the fact that nobody was buying one for me. That was the year I announced that I was going to think of Valentine's Day like Kwanza—a holiday we should all acknowledge, but one that only some people in this country celebrate.

I'm in my mid-thirties and single. I spend my days writing about dating, sometimes writing about writing about dating, and this year I realized I'm tired of the Rant. I don't feel angry at the holiday. Instead, I'm angry at the people who are angry at the holiday.

I remember in my junior high school in Oklahoma, you could have carnations delivered to your valentines—white for friends, pink for people you had a crush on, red for the person you made out with at recess. We didn't overthink the carnation system. Back then we didn't even know carnations were bad flowers.

Now I can't even scrounge up an Anti-Valentine. A guy I've been corresponding with online (it's not as pathetic as it sounds) won't even pass on information about a few Anti–Valentine's Day parties—the latest trend for single people—because he didn't feel like that would be a good first meeting for us. The final nail in the coffin was when my plan to stay home and watch *Temptation Island* was pre-empted by Barbra Streisand's "last televised concert." What's a single heterosexual to do? I finally decided to have a party for my "Single but Optimistic" friends, not to be confused with an Anti–Valentine's Day party, since as of this printing, I am still pro-valentine. And I invite you to join me—not at my party—but in adopting a more hopeful, inclusive stance. We all have people we love, or at least people we'd like to send a white carnation . . . why not celebrate them? And men—do the expected. That can be romantic, too.

chapter seven

HALLOWEENIES: People who break up around Halloween because it's the last stop before the family-filled, gift-mandated, high pressure holidays: Thanksgiving/Christmas/New Year's.

I find Halloween even scarier as an adult than I did as a kid. And it was plenty scary as a kid, because we had the requisite neighborhood bully, Adrian Sullivan*, who was too old for Halloween but wore some lame semblance of a costume anyhow (usually featuring a red Magic Marker–stained undershirt), and just when you were finally old enough to go trick-or-treating without parental guidance, Adrian would ambush you, steal your candy, and disappear.

I still associate Halloween with the vague threat of loss and a boy I won't be able to reason with, only now that boy is not Adrian, it's . . . (*scary music*) the person sleeping next to me!!! I've had several relationships fall apart on Halloween, and not due—as you might imagine—to the pressure of finding matching costumes. I've yet to date anyone willing to be a Raggedy Andy to

*His name has been changed in case he grew up to be a litigious bully.

my Ann, and frankly that's one of the few facts about my relationship past that I'm proud of.

Instead the problem is Halloween's precarious position in the holiday lineup. It's the last strictly "fun" holiday before the heavy hitters (namely Thanksgiving, Christmas/Chanukah and New Year's) and even the most insensitive single knows you can't break up during the Season. But you *can* break up on Halloween.

The Halloweenie sees the Season as an express train to next year, and if he's at all undecided about his relationship, that's a train he'd rather not board. In addition, the Halloweenie knows that *not breaking up* in late October means suffering through Thanksgiving, which usually involves two non-refundable tickets to somewhere like Pittsburgh, where his girlfriend's mother will inevitably express her desire for grandchildren over the wishbone. He might wish he'd simply gone cold turkey, but it's too late. He can't break up on Thanksgiving.

Then Christmas-slash-Chanukah rolls around, and that involves gift giving, something men are not terribly skilled at in the first place. Add to that the hassle of holiday shopping and the possibility of selecting something deemed inadequate, or worse— something *so good* it is paraded around as a symbol of his love, and many men will wish they'd wrapped up the relationship rather than a gift. But only a Grinch would break up at Christmas.

Then it's New Year's Eve, the world's most overpriced and high pressure "date night," which involves serious planning and a midnight kiss that rings in another ringless year for the girlfriend. This is why most Halloweenies would prefer to trick you into breaking up with them rather than treat you to another holiday season.

For all of the reasons above, and a few other goodies (like the fact that Halloween is actually for kids, so the question for thirty-something single women remains: *Do you know where your children are?*) I believe Halloween has edged out Valentine's Day as the Official Worst Holiday for Singles. After several late October heartbreaks I get a little jittery when pumpkins and "fun-size" Milk Duds appear in the supermarket. I feel the Jack-o-lanterns are mocking my holiday hopefulness with a grin that says, "Happy Halloween! We *know* we'll be thrown out in a week. Do you?"

chapter eight

THE MILE HIGH AND DRY CLUB: The reality of flying solo, which is not sex in the bathroom—it's a screaming baby and a couple who wants you to move so they can sit together.

"Hi," he said. He was adorable, and he appeared to have the seat next to mine on the plane. That never happens. I usually end up sitting next to someone with a child, which means either making silly faces for five hours or appearing to be a woman who doesn't like children. I do like children. I want to have some eventually. I just don't want to fly with them.

In fact, I have no political aspirations, but I did once come up with what I think is an excellent program to keep teenage girls from getting pregnant. Give them a baby (preferably one with an earache) for the duration of a cross-country flight. The child's parents could sit in another row and enjoy a little break, the teenager could fly free (an incentive for the teenager and the parents), and the teen pregnancy rate would plummet. It's a good idea, don't you think? If anybody in elected office or in charge of an airline is reading this book, it's yours. All I ask is that you get this program in place before I have a child.

I am somewhat chastised, because last time I flew, I was looking forward to sleeping on the plane, and a woman with a screaming baby got on board and I was thinking, "Please don't let that baby be sitting next to me, please don't let that baby be sitting next to me," and of course, he was sitting next to me. And this baby looked healthy, like he could scream all the way to L.A. and back. His weary mother dropped off a baggie of Cheerios and then looked for an empty overhead compartment in which to put, I hoped, the baby. I took this opportunity to surreptitiously summon a flight attendant, and said that if another seat opened up, I would very much like to move. She nodded sympathetically. Then the woman sat down, let out a big sigh and said, "It's so hard to travel with a baby. When I was pregnant everybody was so nice, and now it's like I'm a pariah." I instantly felt guilty, and overcompensated by pretending to be equally indignant: "It's true. It's a disgrace. Everybody was a baby once. Why aren't people more tolerant?" I spent the rest of the flight praying the flight attendant would *not* offer me that seat I requested. In fact, I felt so remorseful and hypocritical that by the time we were somewhere over Phoenix I was holding the Cheerios and singing "The Itsy Bitsy Spider."

So it was particularly refreshing and startling to see an adorable man about to sit next to me, and even more refreshing to hear him say, "Hi." I was well into visions of the two of us joining the Mile High Club when I realized he was still speaking: "Would you mind switching seats so I can sit with my girlfriend, Candi?" Candi looked at me sweetly. She was predictably blond and thin. Okay, first of all, her name was Candi, so I didn't like her already. Second of all, he didn't *have* to say her name, so obviously he just enjoyed saying it, enjoyed dating a Candi. Third of all, Candi stole my man. And fourth of all (am I allowed four?), I wasn't feeling very supportive of relationships. So I said that. I actually said, "You know, I just broke up with someone, and I'm not feeling very *pro-love* right now, so if you don't mind, I really don't want to switch seats." Candi looked disappointed. I felt like a raving bitch. But I held my ground (and my window seat) because why was I singled out to move? I'll tell you why. Because I'm single! I can sit anywhere! Nobody will miss me!

Candi and her boyfriend smiled at each other wistfully and shrugged. How would they survive apart? Not my problem. I was alone. I was going home for the holidays alone. I had to find a space in long-term parking alone and lug my bags alone to the bus stop alone and take them off the bus alone and wait in the line alone to check in alone, and when I got to my sister's house in Dallas, I would be sleeping on a futon in the baby's room alone. So I figured Candi could be alone for one fucking flight.

Her boyfriend turned out to be a very nice guy. We talked the whole way to Dallas. And we didn't talk about her. She was barely a blip on our radar. When he asked me for a pen, I knew Candi was on the way out. He would give me his number and we would end up together, and the whole thing would make a great story, all because I wouldn't give up my seat.

He wrote "I love you" on his cocktail napkin (which I thought seemed a little premature!) and then he had the people in front of us pass the note to Candi.

How many people must be inconvenienced by this relationship?

As he gave me back my pen, I wished I were sitting next to a screaming baby.

chapter nine

SEASON'S GRIPINGS: The complaints you might lodge after receiving your 200th photo Christmas card featuring the family you've yet to create.

It's that time of year again—the photo Christmas cards are coming! People you barely remember are about to land in your mailbox complete with spouse, children, and possibly a pet. Except for my ex-boyfriends. They continue to amaze me with their inability to commit, which should be some consolation, but it isn't. (It just reminds me that I sure know how to pick 'em.) Here's one ex kissing a dolphin in Hawaii. Here's a form letter from another saying, "I'm in love . . . with myself." He goes on to explain that he's joined the self-help group, the Forum, thinks everybody should, is deliriously happy, call for details.

The rest of the cards are more typical, probably because they are from people I haven't dated, people who have connected successfully, and now they and theirs want to wish me and mine a happy holiday. They mean no harm by this inadvertent postal pressure. But when you're single, especially newly single, the photo Christmas cards can make for a very merry, when-will-I-marry breakdown.

Let's talk about the cards with the babies dressed up like Santa for a minute. Now, I would definitely rather get these by mail than by e-mail. E-mail photos—for those of us who still use dial-up modems—can mean twenty minutes of downloading and several computer crashes. By the time the photo arrives that baby better be pretty damn cute. And it arrives pixel by pixel, so you have to go through the anticipation of . . . it's . . . it's a baby . . . it's a baby in a . . . a baby in a denim jacket . . . a baby in a denim jacket in a . . . in a . . . in a pumpkin patch! Aw, isn't that the cutest thing to ever freeze my computer?

Take it from one who knows, it is virtually impossible to get off a friend's baby photo distribution list without sounding like a complete misanthrope. (It's hard enough to write this piece without sounding that way.) You basically have to change your e-mail address. In fact, it might be helpful to reserve one e-mail address for friends with babies, and then don't check it everyday. Just check once you've had children of your own.

It was last year, right around my fourth baby-dressed-as-Santa photo Christmas card (baby propped uncomfortably on the couch, picture snapped just pre- or post-tantrum) that I decided to buy a sports car.

I needed to do *something* to celebrate my singleness, something frivolous and impractical, something I couldn't do if I had a baby to dress like Santa—so I bought a convertible two-seater. This car was not known for its safety record, and it wouldn't accommodate a baby seat (or even a very tall person), but it was extremely cool. I even opted for the more-fun-to-drive, male-impressing, annoying-during-stop-and-go-traffic stick shift.

Soon after my purchase, I attended a baby shower tea at the Ritz-Carlton in Pasadena. I didn't even know my friends had hats, but there they were in hats eating cucumber finger sandwiches. I remember as I pulled away in my convertible—my expectant friend loading the last gift into her minivan in my rearview mirror—I felt light. Not alone, not single—just free and unencumbered and content.

Sure, I want the rest of it someday. I will probably photograph my kid in a pumpkin patch. I will probably wear a hat. But for now, me and mine (my sports car) wish you and yours whatever makes you happy.

some things to talk about in therapy

chapter ten

IMPOSTER COMPLEX: What a relationship columnist might feel when she is not currently in a relationship, has not been able to maintain a relationship, does not have any prospects for a new relationship, nor does she even have a funny term for this predicament.

I recently got a call from a new editor at *Glamour*. She was taking over the Sexual Ethics column and wanted me to write a piece on the problems of juggling a bunch of men at once. She asked with an optimism that implied she was under thirty, "Are you currently in this situation?" and I paused to let the question die a dignified death before telling her, "No, I'm currently juggling, um, zero," which is precisely why I had stopped contributing to the Sexual Ethics column. I was worried that newly manicured *Glamour* readers from beauty salons around the country were going to rally and expose me as a fraud. Who was I to be giving relationship advice? If I'm so smart, why am I home on Saturday night trying to come up with dating tips?

I should explain that I am in my mid-thirties and divorced for four years. I still believe in love despite all evidence to the contrary, and I believe in soul mates, although lately I've been wondering if mine might be agoraphobic. I'm out there, baby. I'm looking. I own Rollerblades and Spandex. I even read *The Rules* despite the warning that you shouldn't discuss *The Rules* with your therapist, and the fact that the authors' bios were basically, "We're married and you're not."

However, I keep ending up in situations for which there seem to be no rules. For example, I recently had dinner with my ex-husband, who is now gay. (Okay, the politically correct thing to say is that he was always gay, he just didn't know it when I put on the big white dress in front of two hundred of my closest friends.) Despite the bitterness of that last parenthetical I have managed to remain friends with my ex, because he is still one of the finest men I know, and because instead of thinking I somehow turned him gay, I prefer to believe my therapist's romantic notion that he tried to be straight for me, and how many men will do that? (Hopefully just the one.)

So we're at a Chinese restaurant, my gay ex and I, and I pay with my Visa card, which is relevant because it's one of those credit cards with a photo on it, and I used a wedding photo (you can't see the dress) because I couldn't just throw all those pictures away. They're very flattering shots. Anyhow, a sweet elderly couple at a nearby table is smiling at us, and I'm sure they're thinking we're on a date, and I'm getting this morbid urge to tell them the actual situation, but I don't because my ex seems to need my advice, or my go-ahead, or *something* because he's not sure he's as in love as his partner is, and he's wondering what to do because this guy is starting to talk about long-term stuff, and even adopting kids together . . . and I realize as his mouth moves and the elderly couple smiles and my wedding photo is returned on a tray with two fortune cookies, that my ex may have a husband and kids before I do.

So no, I am not currently juggling. I am evaluating, reflecting, and hoping this road less taken is not a dead end. I've been encouraged to write a movie about this, because that's what Los Angeles–based writers do with traumatic yet possibly commercial events, the prevailing attitude being that if a tree falls in a forest and no one makes a movie about it, who cares? The thing is, I'm not sure what the ending should be. I'd like it to involve the arrival of my soul mate—the person I was supposed to be with all along—so we could muse about the circuitous ways of the world, and the credits would roll before we had our first fight. In the meantime, I accepted the *Glamour* assignment, because as a television comedy writer who's always writing for other people, I hate turning down an opportunity to write in my own voice. However, it was hard to write in my own voice given that I was supposed to be writing about juggling and I hadn't so much as kissed a guy in nine months. I began to refer to the piece as my first work of fiction.

The last guy I kissed was an excellent kisser, but it was a classic rebound relationship. He was the polar opposite of my ex-husband, meaning I couldn't talk to him at all, which is something I've come to look for in a man. Communication is a red flag to me now because my ex and I could talk about anything. It was like talking to a girlfriend. (Okay, I was blind.) So just to be on the safe side, my post-divorce relationships have been with aggressively manly men who ignore me for football, know nothing about antique furniture, and for the most part, have no idea what I'm talking about.

When I turned in the first draft of "How to Juggle a Bunch of Men at Once" (which is called "Male Harems" in this collection and was never published until now), I thought it was upbeat and funny, although it's possible I didn't have enough sympathy for the "problems" of the male-juggling women I interviewed. The piece began, *"I am in awe of Lyla."* Lyla was the editor's friend and the woman who inspired the idea. She should have been writing the column, but she's not a writer plus she doesn't have time because she's too busy dating. Anyhow, it began, *"I am in awe of Lyla. She has so many men in her life she had to start keeping notes in her Filofax to avoid getting confused. I'd like to be that confused. I've had one date in the past six months and the only confusing thing about that was why the friend who fixed us up didn't mention the guy was a hemp activist."* The editor had this concern: "I'm afraid this makes you sound undesirable, when the case, really, is that you're being picky, right?"

I thought about it and concluded I'm neither. I have been known to be desirable. And as far as being picky, I was willing to give the hemp activist a second chance despite the fact that he was wearing hemp pants. The truth is, he was the one who didn't call me, so once again, I was left with no balls in the air.

I had another date recently and after dinner the guy said, "You should know, I'm sort of seeing someone," and instead of thinking, "Darn! I like this guy!" all I could think was, "How the hell am I supposed to juggle you now?"

So it has come to this. I am actually juggling a few men. I kissed a guy the other night just to end my slump. I am trying to be open rather than picky, and picky rather than undesirable. I am relying on self-help material I wrote. And my fortune cookie, the night I had dinner with my ex, said nothing about any of this.

chapter eleven

YOUR NUMBER: The actual number of sexual partners you've had over a lifetime, not to be confused with the Number You Give When Asked—which is usually inflated for men and deflated for women.

Two. According to a recent major study of American sexuality, that is the median number of sexual partners women said they'd had over a lifetime. Two! And that's just the median, which means a lot of women said one or zero. It also means I am a total tramp.

I feel torn discussing in print the fact that the number of men I've slept with is higher than that median because a) my parents are still alive and I'm sure they'd prefer to believe I am one of those pristine "ones" or "twos"; and b) those of you who were lucky enough to avoid this much publicized piece of research (*Sex in America: A Definitive Survey*) will now be forced to confront your total, as I was.

But sooner or later, we all have our day of reckoning. Before mine arrived, I never really pondered my number. As a single woman living in Los Angeles, it seemed daunting enough just to find a guy who wasn't gay, married or both; then get him to notice me among all the bustiered blondes on Rollerblades; then resolve conflicts with work schedules, taste in movies, etc. Racking up a few partners along the way seemed incidental—unavoidable, really. But now, thanks to this survey, I can't hear the sound of a condom package ripping open without also hearing the *ch-ching* of my count straying even farther from the median. Clearly, this is no way to live. So I propose the following five-step program, specially designed to help us all come to terms with our number, whatever it may be.

Step one: Dispute the survey. I am not alone in wondering if *Sex in America: A Definitive Survey* is not so definitive after all. Sure, it was conducted over the course of two years by three Ph.D.s, but my girlfriends and I have these questions for the authors: Of the 3,432 people interviewed, how many had their fingers crossed? How many were interviewed with a current boyfriend present?

Step two: Think like a man. My male friends unanimously agree that no matter what the median number of partners was for men (six, according to the study), they themselves would prefer to rank somewhere *above* it. This, I suppose, is not news. When Wilt Chamberlain reported sleeping with 20,000 women, men were less appalled than awestruck. They pulled out calculators and gleefully factored how many women a day—how many at once—would make that number possible. All of which supports the notion that men feel much less guilt about sex than women do. When was the last time you heard a male friend complain, "I wish I hadn't slept with her," or "We really should have waited?" I know what you're thinking: Society has different standards for men. But attitudes seem to be changing. Want proof? Perform the next step.

Step three: Rent *Four Weddings and a Funeral.* If only more of us could feel as comfortable with our number as Andie MacDowell's character did in this hit comedy. Over tea with Hugh

Grant, she unapologetically recalled all thirty-three of the men she'd slept with, and Hugh Grant's character found it impressive! Most of my friends expressed doubt that the average Joe would be as receptive as Hugh was to this sexual tally, but in reality the problem is not men judging us—it's us judging ourselves.

Step four: Get tested. It's quite possible that your concerns about your number stem from a deeper anxiety—a fear that you haven't practiced safe sex as zealously as you should have in this age of AIDS. There's only one way to get past this fear: Get tested for HIV. It's scary, but ultimately you're better off knowing. Most likely you'll receive a clean bill of health; then you can stop feeling guilty, buy a megapack of condoms and get on with your life.

Step five: Adopt a different numerical system. If you've been safe and responsible all along, but your number still makes you uneasy, fret not. Just as the metric system is an alternate way of measuring, I suggest the "hindsight system" as an alternate way of counting sexual partners.

Using the hindsight system, you count only the partners with whom you were emotionally as well as sexually involved because those, after all, are the men that really mattered. Say you wish you'd lost your virginity to someone other than number one because number one was a guy you met at a frat party and never talked to again. (This did not happen to me, Mom. It's just an example.) Now, with hindsight, you can pick the guy you wish had been number one—your first love, perhaps—and start counting from there. You may also omit anyone who said he'd call and still hasn't. And ignore anyone identified by a location instead of a name (for example, Club Med Bora-Bora guy). But while you are conducting your recount, be aware of roughly how many partners you now regret. You can't entirely erase those people from your past, but you can make an effort to avoid them in the future. Wait longer. Say no more often. Test your brakes occasionally.

One day, ideally, you meet the guy who gives you a reason to stop counting. If that day has yet to arrive, and all of the above fail you, here's one last suggestion: Start tracking down old boyfriends so that you can keep your number where it is and still have some fun.

chapter twelve

CARMUNICATION: The language used by fathers when communicating with their adult daughters, basically consisting of the phrase, "How's the car?"

There are two things I can count on my dad asking every time he calls me in Los Angeles from my hometown in Oklahoma: "Is there anything I can do for you?" and "How's the car?" I suspect he asks what he can do for me because his father (an air force major) was never really there for him, and he's doggedly determined to provide my sister and me with the support he lacked. Throughout my youth he never missed a Bluebirds' dinner, dance recital, school play, softball game, graduation, or father-daughter sorority weekend. In fact, he was so supportive, I occasionally longed for one of those dads who dressed better and cared less, but that was not to be. My dad would forever be the guy wearing shorts with dress shoes and black socks, cheering me on, expecting greatness.

His other standard question, "How's the car?" used to strike me as a waste of long-distance dollars from a man who once suggested making a list of what you want to talk about before calling someone out of state. (This, as far as I can tell, was supposed to prevent you from digressing into an actual conversation.) What I've come to realize is that "How's the car?" is not about the car. It's a father's way of asking his adult daughter how she is. The advantage is that if there's something wrong with the car, he knows what you should do and approximately how much it should cost, whereas if you're having marital problems or doubting your career choice, he might have to put Mom on the phone.

My friend Jenny said she always gets the "How's the car?" question from her dad. "It's the only way he knows how to communicate," she says. Her family often jokes that her dad, a successful New York lawyer, shows his love for others by helping them buy used cars. "His form of love is the classifieds. He does all the research, talks to random people in Queens, drives to random boroughs. It would be easier to say 'I love you,'" she muses.

Another friend, Chris, said that when she called her parents in Long Island after the 1994 Northridge earthquake, her car was the first thing her dad asked about. "It was 4:30 A.M. here in Los Angeles. Both of them got on the phone at the same time. I said I was okay, but the phone lines were jammed so I had to make it short, and in the few sentences I allowed them to get in, my dad managed to ask about the car," she says. "He was concerned whether it was parked under the building and if so, had the building fallen on it? I hadn't even been outside yet, but when I didn't have the answer, I felt like a bad daughter, so I called a couple days later with the car report."

My car report usually consists of me saying, "It's fine," because I've always owned very reliable cars that came strongly recommended by *Consumer Reports*. I know this not because I've ever bought an issue of *Consumer Reports*, but because my dad copies, highlights, and mails me the relevant research each time I'm in the market for a new set of wheels. He actually flew out to help me buy my two previous cars, reasoning that the plane fare was justified if he could use his accounting skills to save me money and keep me from being lured by the siren song of financing.

At age thirty I finally took the plunge into adulthood by leasing a car without his help or advice. I guess I was curious to see how the experience would go if I went in *not* thinking everyone was trying to take advantage of me. (My father went ballistic when the paperwork arrived on my previous car and the monthly payment was a penny more than we had agreed to pay. I think it was at that moment, as he told our weary salesman, "See? This is what I hate!" that I decided to shop for my next car alone.) I ended up leasing an Infiniti I3o, which involved three trips to the auto mall, a search for the elusive blue book, a trade-in and an annoying salesman named Jimmy Carter ("Not the president!"). The whole thing seemed unnecessarily complicated, and I'm still not sure if I got a good deal, but at least I asserted my automotive independence. Sort of. In a moment of weakness I decided to bring along my boyfriend, and I knew I had once again surrendered control when I heard him say we wouldn't sign unless Jimmy threw in a couple of Infiniti baseball caps.

In retrospect, I'm sure my dad was hurt rather than proud that I ventured into a car dealership without consulting him first. Although a daughter's independence is evidence of a job well done, it still implies the job's done, and many fathers are reluctant to retire. My dad is overworked and understaffed at his accounting office, but he'd happily hop on a plane if I said I needed his help. His frequent question, "Is there anything I can do for you?" underlines the fact that he wishes there was still something tangible he could provide. It's interesting to me that even though we're tied by blood and I love him no matter what, he still seems to need a concrete function (suggesting stocks, finding the cheapest plane fare, paying for dinner) in order to feel like he has a role in my life.

I noted this for the first time when my parents and I drove to Door County, Wisconsin, the weekend after my college graduation. Door County is full of everything a dad hates—dress shops, quaint restaurants, and antique stores. My recollection of my dad in an antique store is of him holding up a creamer in the shape of a cow and calling out to my mom, "We had one of these and we threw it out!" We arrived late at night in a town called Egg Harbor, and my dad rose at the crack of dawn to drive around and get the lay of the land. That way when my mom and I woke up, he could be the expert. I guess in his mind, he was the lion looking for a safe watering hole for his cubs. He had to prove he was still needed, especially since I was about to move to New York for my first real job. New York City . . . where you don't need a car.

Given the history I have with my dad, I knew it wouldn't be easy to tell him two years ago I wanted to switch accountants. He'd been doing my taxes all my life, but as my career progressed, I realized I was uncomfortable with the idea that my father knew exactly what I was making. I also liked the idea of having an accountant who had other writer clients, who lived in my city and who wouldn't have a heart attack if he knew what I was paying my agent, lawyer, and housekeeper. It was a move toward increased independence. I was ready to take off the training wheels. I wasn't sure, however, if my dad was ready to let go of the bike.

I worried for a long time about how and when to bring this up, then I finally decided I was overthinking it. I should be able to be honest, if not in person, at least in a letter. The result was the most carefully written letter in the history of correspondence. Peace treaties have been hammered out with less attention to detail. I read drafts to my boyfriend and my therapist. I reread and revised. I finally mailed it, and at some point between leaving my house and arriving at my parents', my carefully constructed letter became a declaration of war. My dad wouldn't talk to me for a week. My mom did her best to run interference, assuring me I should do what I want with my life (and my 1040), but she couldn't reason with my dad. As far as he was concerned, I was firing him not only as my accountant, but also as my father. Finally we spoke, and he voiced his real concern: What would we talk about if not my tax questions? Would I call as often if I didn't need him for financial advice? I assured him we would have plenty of other things to talk about. Maybe this would finally free us up to talk about things that matter. Life. Love. There was a long silence on the line. Then finally, thankfully, he said he understood, that he respected what I was trying to do, and that he loved me—although he didn't use those words. What he said was: "So . . . how's the car?"

chapter thirteen

RELATIONSHIP RERUNS: A sobering stage (usually occurring around age thirty) when you realize that the men you meet are basically repeats of the men you've already dated.

You know you're in the metaphorical summer of your soul mate search when you turn on the charm and all you can find are reruns. Not reruns in the sense that you've actually been out with this particular man before (although my friend Ellen claims she's been dating so long that she was set up with someone a second time, and unfortunately they didn't realize this until they were on their déjà date). But that's not what I'm talking about. I'm also not talking about running into ex-boyfriends because a) recycling is good for the environment and b) ex-boyfriends are too easy to recognize. Relationship reruns are much more subversive. They sneak up on you in the form of a fresh suitor who slowly reminds you of an ex-boyfriend until you realize you've already been there, done that, lived that episode of your life.

I first noticed I was in relationship reruns after I broke up with a guy who, at thirty-two, lived with his parents and didn't have a checking account. (Note: He didn't live with his parents when I met him. He lived with a roommate . . . who was dealing drugs, and that's why he moved out, and okay, pretty much any way you slice it I look like someone who should not be doling out dating advice.) The point is I did finally break up with him, because he wasn't even looking for his own place, and I didn't want to always have to be the responsible one. A few months later I threw a party for my single friends and their single friends, and somebody's single friend was flirting with me, which was, of course, the whole point of the party. Over cocktails and artichoke dip he told me that he was a screenwriter who house-sits a fabulous home (read: doesn't pay rent), and that his last girlfriend broke up with him because she wanted him to get his own place, and she obviously didn't understand the life of a struggling screenwriter, and did I want to go to lunch some time? All I could think was: "We've been to lunch. I've already dated you." My party epiphany: It's tempting to settle for a rerun when there's nothing else on, but if you recognize some of the lines, and you know how it turns out, why waste your time? Especially if that particular episode of your life was not so great the first time.

It's tempting—it's *always* tempting—to blame men or the lack thereof, to conclude the single ones are all the same, or at least the same type, or several types but you've dated one of each. But after a certain number of rerun run-ins, you have to consider whether *you* might be the one stuck in a rut. Maybe it's true that you get what you put out there (or whom you put out for). Not many women I know would have dated a guy who had no checking account, who had to drive to the phone company to pay his bill in dollar bills, so maybe it's no surprise that I continued to attract others like him. Maybe in order to avoid reruns you have to re-program your VCR (Various Crappy Relationships), get off the couch (unless it's your therapist's), and open yourself up to a new season of men.

chapter fourteen

TAFFETA ENVY: The secret desire to be a bridesmaid, aggravated by the fact that women who are frequent bridesmaids love to complain about it.

There are three numbers that I, as a woman, have trouble admitting: the number of men I've slept with, my weight, and the number of times I've been a bridesmaid.

I may never admit the actual number of men I've slept with. I'm not so much embarrassed that it's a high number as I am mortified that due to some beer-laden college years, it might be inexact.

As for my weight, I actually passed on bungee jumping in New Zealand not because I was afraid to dive off a suspension bridge with a rubber band around my ankles, but because before you jump, they weigh you and write your weight in bold numbers on your hand. They do this, I was told, not to humiliate people, but because lying about your weight could lead to almost certain death. My weight (even in kilos) is not a small number. I cling to the "big boned" theory, although a friend of mine recently had a bout with breast cancer, and to add insult to injury, her x-rays revealed that she has a very delicate frame. The doctors were able to save her breast, but she has permanently lost her "big boned" excuse, which may be equally important to one's womanhood.

Still, my most embarrassing statistic is the number of times I've been a bridesmaid, and not because that number is high. I have heard the lament: "Always a bridesmaid, never a bride," but I suffer from a rarer malady: "Always a guest book person, never a bridesmaid."

Yes, I have been a guest book person, a psalm reader, a reader of my own poem, a flower petal distributor, a program passer outer, and—before we knew it was a problem for the birds—a keeper of the rice. But rarely have I been awarded that purple heart of friendship that would put me among the few, the proud, the bridesmaids. I find this distressing. I always considered myself a good friend, a "girl's girl," but the lack of taffeta in my closet would seem to imply otherwise.

The truth is I have only been a bridesmaid twice.

And once was my sister. I must have protested a little too vocally about the green satin bow-on-the-butt dress she made me wear, because I was only asked to be in one other wedding after that. That was my friend Kristy's (and she was one of my bridesmaids, so she might have felt obligated). I suppose I didn't do so well at her wedding either, because a) I got lost in my rental car on the way to the reception, thus missing the photos and toasts, and b) it was a very Christian wedding, and at one point during the ceremony I thought we were singing "Edelweiss," but it turns out everyone else was singing "Jesus Christ" to the tune of "Edelweiss," and my moment of realization was captured on video.

So maybe I'm not cut out to be a bridesmaid. Maybe you only get two shots before you are sentenced to a life of guest bookdom, and as Miranda said in a *Sex and the City* episode I wrote, "It's a bullshit job, Carrie. People know what to do with a guest book."

I have a few theories, which are slightly more palatable than the "I'm a B-list friend" theory. One is that because I'm bi-coastal it's hard to maintain friendships on either coast. I ran this by my screenwriting agent and she said she has a friend who was fixed up by Elle MacPherson, and this woman's biggest reservation was, "What if it works out—will I have to have Elle MacPherson as a bridesmaid? How could I look beautiful next to Elle Mac-Pherson?" So Elle MacPherson probably never gets to be a bridesmaid either, my agent mused. This, of course, has nothing to do with me, but it illustrates why she's a good agent.

A theory that *might* apply to me is that, as in matters of love, my timing might be off. My high school girlfriends were closer with their college friends when they got married, and my college friends were closer with their local friends when they got married, and my local (L.A. and N.Y.) friends are having as much trouble finding a husband as I am. In fact, most of my closest female friends are like the characters on our show—smart, funny, ambitious women whose quest for love takes them so far into their thirties and forties, the big wedding no longer seems necessary or appropriate. Some even elope, which doesn't help me out at all. Others choose to have intimate ceremonies in remote locations, and I'm honored to be one of the few guests, but what about *my* needs?

I do have a handful of girlfriends who could still boost my stat if they steer clear of men with too many sisters, although I recently lost one ace-in-the-hole (another of my bridesmaids) when she realized she was a lesbian. In theory, a lesbian wedding could mean *twice* the number of bridesmaids, but I'm not holding my breath. It also occurred to me that if all else fails, I could cast myself as a bridesmaid in my own wedding. This might make the interesting statement that a woman can be her own best friend. Or it might just seem confusing and pathetic.

So I'm putting the word out: I am available for weddings. And as a *bridesmaid*, I'm practically a virgin.

dating up a storm

chapter fifteen

MALE HAREMS: An idea whose time has come; the many men you can juggle once you genuinely *stop* looking for a commitment.

I was in awe of Lyla. She had so many men in her life she had to keep notes in her Filofax to avoid getting confused. I wanted to be that confused. I'd had one date in the past six months and the only confusing thing about that was why the friend who fixed us up didn't mention the guy was a hemp activist. Perhaps if there were other men in my life, I thought, that date would have been just one colorful episode among many colorful episodes rather than the crystallization of my fear that if I do have a soul mate, he got hit by a bus.

Lyla does not have these thoughts. She is far too busy dating, providing further proof that juggling is the way to go. But how do you get started? Lyla and other successful jugglers shared their advice and I tried it (because I'm *that* committed to research) and it worked.

First, find a harem of men. Okay, nobody actually said this, but it was a question that kept coming up in my mind. How do you find multiple men to date when most single women I know are hard pressed to find one guy they want to meet for coffee? The trick is to remember these men don't have to be The One. In fact, by definition they won't be. They will be One of the Guys You're Dating, and this cavalier attitude actually brings the men to you. They may not show up on your doorstep like the newspaper, but if you're open to meeting new people, and go places where that could conceivably happen, and tell your friends you're ready to be set up, you'll be turning men away. I was dubious about this, as I'm sure you are. You're thinking, "My friends never fix me up." That's because they think you're looking for your future husband, and finding your future husband is a lot of pressure. Once you make it clear that you just want to date around, you'll be surprised how many single men your friends know.

Make a list; check it twice. It became clear Lyla needed a system when she started confusing the friends and stories of her various and sundry men. For example, her date mentioned his friend, Joe, and she asked, "Is he the tall guy who only dates tall women?" and her date had no idea who she was talking about. Now she avoids that embarrassment by making a few notes after a night out. These relationship CliffsNotes help her remember details like where the guy went to college, where he works, where he's from, how he tipped, taste in music, and red flags like too much enthusiasm for *Beavis and Butt-head.*

I decided to try this out when I got home from the blind date that was supposed to kick off my juggle-fest. The date itself was decidedly fireworks-free, but on paper the guy didn't sound so bad, so an added bonus might be that by writing down you avoid writing off. Remember you're not looking for Mr. Right. You're looking for a few good Mr. Maybes. The main goal in the beginning is just to get some balls in the air.

Categorize your clothes. Getting ready for a date can be tough enough, let alone getting ready for multiple dates in one week. Jenny, who at her peak was juggling three men in Los Angeles and one in New York, suggests designating a first, second, and daytime date outfit. That way you don't have to waste time trying to remember what you wore with whom. Believe it or not, you will have this problem.

Avoid same-name men. Okay, yes, as my bachelor neighbor Nick points out, this does reduce the risk of calling out the wrong name in a moment of passion, but in general it's very confusing to date two people with the same first name. I know this because in my quest to experience juggling, I ended up dating two Steves at once. Luckily they had very different voices, so on the phone I could sort it out after a few neutral questions, but messages became the bane of my existence. My pleasant relationship with the office receptionist disintegrated into moments of desperation and blame. "Call *which* Steve?" I would cry, waving the pink while-you-were-out slip. "I don't care if he said I'd know who it was. Next time get a number!" It finally became clear that I had one Steve too many when I unwittingly said to a co-worker, "No, I'm talking about the *good* Steve."

Use nicknames for easy reference. If *you're* having trouble keeping your love life straight, imagine how your friends feel. Nicknames make it easier for everyone to follow the saga of Swing Dance Man, Lousy Tipper, Hemp Activist, Bad Hair Guy, and the Good Steve.

Give 'em the sushi test. Although Lyla likes to let the guy choose the restaurant to see what he comes up with, my friend Paula has another strategy that makes dating more of a controlled experiment. She meets every first date at her favorite sushi restaurant. "It's like my home ground," she says. At least she knows she'll like the meal, and by sitting at the bar she can get the opinion of the sushi chef, who gives her a nod if he approves of the guy.

Observe the "three strikes, you're out" rule. When a Mr. Maybe becomes a Mr. Why Didn't I Stay Home and Rent a Movie, the experienced juggler's attitude is: "Next!" As Jenny says, "Keep moving. Put another guy in the slot when one drops out." Lyla says some of her friends think she's getting too picky, but she's confident there are other fish in the sea. Paula's so confident she eliminates men who don't *eat* fish.

Dating around doesn't mean sleeping around. A male friend who juggles like a pro explained that for men, the point of juggling is the sexual smorgasbord, to sleep with as many women as possible—otherwise you might as well be in a relationship. Women—no shock—seemed to have more scruples when it came to sex, with the exception of my cousin Sheila who was seeing three men at once and sleeping with all three. "Men have been doing it for years," she said. "I'm forty-nine years old. I'm going to enjoy myself!"

Most women felt it would be tough (not to mention kind of sleazy) to be sleeping with more than one guy, because we all know that once sex is introduced, it's hard not to get attached. Even sleeping with just one of the men you're dating could be asking for trouble. Wouldn't you have a problem with a man who was taking you to dinner but sleeping with someone else? For women juggling is most useful in the early courting stages. I found that it actually helps you slow things down (remember kisses at the door?) so you can really see what's out there.

Be as honest as you wanna be. I asked my male friend, the pro juggler, what he thought about honesty. Is it important to tell people you're dating around? "Not necessary," he said. He explained that unless a man says otherwise, you should assume he's dating around, even sleeping around. This is not the same as lying, he contends, because if confronted he would admit to seeing other women. The thing is, most women don't ask. I was impressed with his guilt-free approach until he added that if I was going to quote him, he'd prefer to remain anonymous. Hmmm.

Lyla advocates full disclosure. She believes in telling a guy early on that she's seeing other people. Not only does it feel more honest; it can actually be a turn-on. For example, she was out with girlfriends one night and a guy asked her what she was doing for New Year's Eve. "I told him I have these four guys I'm juggling and the whole story," she says, "and he asked if he could be the fifth."

When I met the Good Steve he wasn't looking for a relationship because he was thinking of leaving town for business school. The old me (looking for Mr. Right) would have cut my losses and dismissed him, but the new me (the Juggler) simply said, "No problem. I'm not looking for a relationship. I'm just dating around." It wasn't a tactic; it was true, and because of that, I think the Good Steve felt okay about getting involved. A year-and-a-half later he was going to school locally and we were dating exclusively, which leads me to another important piece of advice. . . .

Know when to stop. The trick to successful juggling seems to be not caring. Not faking not caring, but genuinely not caring. This is a problem if and when you fall for someone. Jenny warned me that initially you should fight the urge to date one person exclusively. Continuing to juggle for a while not only makes you more appealing, it keeps you from getting hooked on a man before you truly get to know him.

I had the opportunity to test this theory when I fell very hard, very quickly for the Other Steve. He talked a great game, but he was still seeing an old girlfriend. Following Jenny's advice, I opted not to invite him to a party as my "plus one." Instead I invited a brand new prospect, the Good Steve, because he was cute and nice, and at the very least I knew he was someone I'd like to have as a friend. We ended up having a great time—my friends loved him, he was fun to dance with, he made me laugh—and I would have missed the boat completely if I'd stopped juggling too early and dedicated myself to the Other Steve.

The Good Steve wasn't the least bit threatened by the thought of me dating other men. It was instructive to see how appealing confidence can be, and it made me realize that maybe women shouldn't run the other way when a man doesn't immediately want to become exclusive. Eventually everybody gets tired of juggling. In my case it happened because I realized there was only one person I wanted to kiss goodnight and I didn't need CliffsNotes to remember what I loved about him. Even if he doesn't turn out to be The One, I'm glad I tried juggling. It improved my self-esteem, my understanding of men, and my love life. However, the return to monogamy improved my relationship with the receptionist.

chapter sixteen

GETAWAY BAR: The back-up plan a single should have in place in case it becomes necessary to escape a bad (usually blind) date.

My friend Kate and I went out to dinner last night, and we came up with what might just be a brilliant idea: to open a bar where you could go after a bad date. We don't really care if *we* open this bar. We just think *somebody* should, because the only thing worse than a bad coffee date at 7 P.M. (other than extending it into a bad dinner date) is going home alone at 8 P.M.

I know this is a good idea because it still sounded like a good idea the next morning (which is more than I can say for most of the men I've agreed to go out with lately), and also because instead of doing our respective jobs, Kate and I have been e-mailing each other all day with additional ideas for our bar. Here is what we have so far:

There would definitely be an open-mic area where you could rant about your date ("He didn't ask me one question all night!") while other disgruntled daters cheer you on and try to top you.

You could bring in CDs and request any personal favorite song you need to hear. I would choose "This Year's Love (Had Better Last)" by David Gray.

Anybody who was unfortunate enough not only to endure a bad date but to pay for it would get a free stiff drink upon producing the dinner-for-two receipt. These receipts would be posted like job rejections all over the bar, proving that bad dates are not only common, they are driving the economy.

For women there would be comfort food, fattening and messy dishes like cake and spaghetti, the kind of stuff we pretend not to be interested in on dates. For men there would be a putting green where they could talk about golf (instead of feelings) and take out their frustrations on a little white ball.

The bartenders would be licensed therapists, but not the kind who challenge you too much, because nobody needs to follow a bad date with the suggestion that it failed because you're looking for a mother/father figure.

The bar would actually be a nice place to meet people, because everybody would at least be out there trying, which means you have *something* in common, not to mention that misery loves company. We're not sure what would happen if both unhappy parties were to show up after a bad date. If nothing else, it would be an interesting He Said, She Said situation at the mic. Some names we're considering are:

Getaway Bar

Plan B

The Escape Hatch

The Eject Button

Chasers

B.D. (Bad Date)

After Party

Somewhere To Be (as in "I wish I had more time, but I have Somewhere To Be.")

Kate likes the idea of Plan B, because it's not only Plan B for the patrons, it's Plan B for us. We expected to be happily married with kids by now rather than opening a bar, but isn't life funny? (Isn't Life Funny is a name we rejected, along with I'm Done Dating and Bitter.)

chapter seventeen

CUPIDITY: The faulty logic that leads a well-meaning but clueless third party to believe that two random singles are perfect for each other.

I've been thinking a lot about my friend Mitch. When I was living in New York right out of college he fixed me up with the man I married. Mitch loved to brag about how he brought us together. My father even toasted him at the wedding. Now I am divorced, my ex is dating men, and I have the occasional urge to punch Mitch in the nose.

Of course it's not Mitch's fault that my husband and I turned out to be what self-help books delicately term a "mixed-orientation couple." But now that I'm back in the dating world, I can't help thinking that fixing people up is not something to be taken lightly.

Those who indulge in this practice, however, often do so with little forethought or follow-through. Someone (usually a friend who saw *Sleepless in Seattle* one time too many) will greet you at the water cooler or treadmill, and after listening to you vent about the scarcity of quality men, will say the words that have launched every disastrous blind date in history: "I know a guy—he's perfect for you."

I'm not suggesting this *yenta*-fest should stop. Fix-ups are a necessary evil for most of the busy single people I know. But just as the automotive industry has adopted features like the driver's side air bag, I think we should adopt some safety guidelines for setting people up.

First, I'd advise prospective matchmakers to try to pair up people who have more in common than the fact that they're both single. Or vegetarian. Or from Minnesota. Jenny, who is five-foot-one, complains that she's always being fixed up with short men. "Other than shortness, we have nothing in common. I guess people think we'll look cute together—like matching trolls," she says.

Cynthia, a New York defense attorney, says she's a successful Cupid because she makes compatibility her top priority. She tries to truly understand what her friends are looking for and then give them what they want. For example, she knows a New York City woman who will only go out with men who live in Manhattan. No 718 (Brooklyn) or 201 (New Jersey) area codes need apply. "No, people shouldn't have such attitudes," Cynthia says, "but I'm not going to try to change them with a blind date." She also believes in full disclosure: If the woman is a chain-smoker, or the guy is a little too into golf, you'd better say so up front.

Many of us, in our zeal to make the date happen, oversell the people involved. They are your friends, of course you think they're great, but it's safer to consciously downplay their attributes—and to be completely honest about appearance. That way the couple avoids that awkward letdown at the door when he realizes she's a *hand* model. By the same token, you don't have to emphasize compatibility so much that you end up coaching the date from the sidelines. Let them discover their shared interests on their own. You can't bulletproof the evening.

And now for some firm guidance on who not to fix up:

People you work with. Watch out—the guy who is a real hoot at the office might turn out to be a terrible womanizer, changing your role from benevolent matchmaker to pimp. Or you may learn that the sweet co-worker in the cubicle next to yours sometimes likes to be spanked. That's the kind of more-than-you-needed-to-know information people share when you're the one who arranged the date.

A new friend with an old one. Yes, some are silver and some are gold, and like jewelry, they don't necessarily go together. If you pair up a new friend with an old friend and the date fails miserably, you could be left with the blame and some very awkward dinner parties.

Any man you like too much. Maybe he's an ex-boyfriend. Maybe you're married and you've got a not-so-harmless crush on the guy. One thing is for sure: Nothing clarifies your feelings like seeing him with the woman you brought into his life. My friend Wendy set up a guy she had dated a year earlier. The night of the date, Wendy was out of town and he was house-sitting for her. He called the next morning to tell her how well it had gone. They even made out! At her house? Yes! On her couch? Of course! The whole thing hit a little too close to home, and Wendy realized she wasn't just a disinterested third party. Her new rule: "Make sure you really want to see these people together, because they may end up that way."

In short, setting people up is almost as perilous as actually going on a blind date. It's fine to play Cupid, just don't shoot yourself in the foot.

chapter eighteen

SEVENTEEN DATES: After a breakup, the approximate number of bad dates you have to endure before you have a good one.

He had just left my apartment and I was finally coming to terms with the fact that our relationship—one I truly believed would last forever—was over, that we were breaking up, and that this breakup was final (as evidenced by the ceremonial Returning of the Apartment Key). It was awful. I was heartbroken. Then something odd happened. I heard myself telling my friend Joey that I was going to get back on that horse. I didn't feel like nursing my wounds. Tomorrow I was going to start dating.

I know, of course, that it takes time to get through a heartache, but my thinking (if you can call any mental process that the day of a breakup) was that I had already stayed in this relationship too long, and then the many breakups and makeups took another full year, and I just wanted to *contain the spill*. I couldn't afford to waste any more time. I wanted to have children someday, and I didn't want their birth to be considered a *medical miracle*. I didn't want to be news: Woman has baby at ninety-two! I just wanted to find the idiot I was supposed to marry and get on with it.

Joey listened patiently, and then she said something daunting and prophetic: "Just remember, you're going to have to go on like seventeen bad dates before you have a good one."

I knew she was right. If anything, I worried her estimate was a little conservative. Only in the movies does the girl get to rebound right into the arms of her next great love. In life you have to kiss a few more frogs before you find anybody with prince potential, and seventeen frogs sounded like a decent estimate.

So I decided to get started. I knew from past breakups that I'd be miserable for a while, so why not get my bad dates out of the way *while* I was miserable, I reasoned. Otherwise I'd have to be miserable twice. I enlisted the help of everyone I knew, letting them know that I was available and ready to be fixed up, and that I was *expecting* to have a terrible time, so all pressure was off. In addition, I decided to drop whatever standards I had left and try an online dating service or two. The more the merrier. The point of this exercise was quantity over quality.

I hesitate to describe each of my seventeen dates because I hate to put you through that, and frankly, I have tried so hard to forget. At one point when I was knocking out three dates a week, my friend and co-worker, Michael Patrick King, said it seemed like I wasn't so much dating as doing push-ups. Here are the highlights:

The whole thing started with a bang. Literally. It wasn't really a date (this was a constant debate—what constitutes a date?) but for my purposes, Date #1 was a friend of a friend who was also just getting over a relationship. We were out with a big group, but the two of us eventually bonded over how miserable we were, had a few beers, then went back to my place and made out on the couch. I finally said, "Well, I have to get up early," which he took to mean, "So hurry up and get naked," and that misunderstanding resulted in the aforementioned bang. He stayed the night, but he was a snorer, so I barely slept, which was annoying because I did, in fact, have to get up early to drive in the snow to my friend's mother's funeral. Note: The only thing worse than bad wish-you-were-my-ex sex is not being able to talk about it because you're at a funeral.

Date #2 was approximately half my height and weight and had every single *Seinfeld* episode on tape. Date #3 was not really a date, but I'm counting him because he was my New Year's Eve midnight kiss when a bunch of us escaped from Canyon Ranch to go salsa dancing. Date #3.5 was my ex, and my friends said he *did not count* and that I should actually lose a few dates just for seeing him again, but I settled on the .5 system.

Date #4 was a stand-up comic I kissed in Times Square after having a burger at Joe Allen's, and because he seemed like a nice guy I admitted I was very "reboundy," and we talked openly and honestly for thirty blocks until all hope of romance was lost forever. Date #5 was actually my second date with Date #2, who seemed even shorter than I remembered, and we had sushi at his favorite place, and he kept calling the sushi chef by name. Yellowtail, Kaz. Thank you, Kaz.

Dates #5.5 and #5.75 were my ex. I know I know I know I know.

Date #6 was my second date with Date #1, and it was a real date this time (dinner and everything), but he was still very much on the rebound, whereas I was almost completely over my ex . . . as far as anybody knew.

Date #7 told me over matzoh ball soup that his favorite movie of all time was *Eyes Wide Shut*. I hated *Eyes Wide Shut*. I asked him to take me home.

Date #8 was Benicio Del Toro. Date #9 . . . okay, yes, I suppose I need to explain Date #8. I was at a Golden Globes after party, and *Sex and the City* had won for best comedy, so I had an award but no date. Across the room was Benicio Del Toro, and he had won Best Leading Actor, and he also did not have a date. So I told my friends that I was going to talk to Benicio, and they smiled and told me to have another cocktail. I finally got to Benicio and I told him I loved him in *Traffic*, and he told me he loved *Sex and the City*, and as we were chatting and holding our awards a photographer gestured that he wanted to take our picture, and to my friends' surprise and amazement, Benicio put his arm around me. Then to *my* surprise and amazement, I smiled as the picture was being taken and said *out loud*, "Me and Benicio." I didn't mean to say it out loud. I thought I was just thinking it, but my inner monologue had come out, which is something that can happen when you realize you are not even halfway through your seventeen bad dates. I am aware the Benicio incident doesn't really qualify as a date (at the very least, I suppose the man should have an *inkling* he might be on a date), but it does qualify in that it involved a single man and it was highly embarrassing.

Date #9 was a fix-up who sent back his rack of lamb because it was "disappointing" and who smoked, but didn't carry his own cigarettes so he was forced to bum them off random annoyed people he thought he was bonding with. I remember there were two women at the table next to us laughing and catching up, and I was thinking, I used to be those women and I used to wish I was on a date, and now I am on a date and I would give anything to be those women.

Date #10 was a brunch date because I was done with dinner dates. He was a network television executive who grew up in London, according to his online profile. He didn't have his picture posted because he said he didn't want people to recognize him. I found out (upon asking him about his childhood in London) that he never lived in London. He actually grew up in South Africa, but there aren't a lot of South African network execs, and he didn't want people to "figure it out." He also lied about his last name (same reason) and it turned out he was a network *Standards and Practices* executive, which means his job is basically telling writers, "You can't say that!" So anyone who watches *Sex and the City* can see why this was not a great match.

Now I don't mean to brag, but my job is pretty high profile, and I was online with my real hometown and my picture for all to see. So I told him, "It's possible there's not as much intrigue around your social life as you think there is." He laughed, and he actually turned out to be a fairly smart, sensitive man, which prompted me to answer honestly when he asked about my last relationship, and before I knew it I was crying in my omelette right in front of whoever the hell he was.

Date #11 was at least honest, but he seemed witty and sarcastic in his e-mails, and in person he just seemed bitter. And I was trying to avoid bitter people, because after eleven bad dates I was highly susceptible. Date #12 was a cute online prospect named Josh, but over pizza I accidentally called him Joel, making me wonder if I should slow down a bit.

On Valentine's Day I received two dozen long-stem red roses with no card, which was a problem because at that point they could have been from anyone in the Tri-State area. They turned out to be from my ex. I decided it was a test and I had to press on. I did not get this far to end up right back where I started.

Date #13 was a plastic surgeon taking a golf clinic at Chelsea Piers who had a house in the Hamptons and used to date a stewardess and asked if I was "swimsuit ready."

Date #14 was too young and too close to his parents, but he did seem to have good taste in music, and that's how I came up with the idea of the first-date CD exchange, so even if the date wasn't great, both parties would at least get a new CD.

In my journal under Date #15 I wrote, "Oh God, let this be over!" (This was not so much a reflection of him as it was the cumulative effect of fifteen bad dates.) He seemed very thrown by my request that he bring a CD, and he brought ABBA's *Greatest Hits* (not, I suspect, because it's kitchy fun, but because it's the first CD you'll find alphabetically). I brought him *Deuces Wild*, a B. B. King duet compilation album, which he tucked into his backpack as if I'd just publicly given him a condom. It's important for you to understand that when we spoke on the phone, he claimed he was a Ping-Pong fan, and I love Ping-Pong, so I figured that was as good a date as any. (I also liked that it wouldn't involve another meal since I was not, in fact, swimsuit ready.) It was clear there was no chemistry, but that I was used to. I was more annoyed that Date #15 wasn't very good at Ping-Pong, because I *am* pretty good at Ping-Pong, and you can't have a decent game if you aren't evenly matched. I was ready to call it an afternoon when I overheard the guy at the table behind us bragging about how he was a "Ping-Pong machine" and he was "made to win at Ping-Pong," and I love to trash talk Ping-Pong, so I said, "I bet I could beat you," and my date said, "I'll bet you twenty dollars she can beat you."

I played the "machine," and easily won two games in a row. My date left with twenty bucks in his pocket (he didn't even offer to share!) and a very good CD. I left with ABBA's *Greatest Hits* and the feeling that I had been pimped out for Ping-Pong.

By Date #16 I hit a wall—the kind marathon runners talk about. I had already whittled my dates down to coffee and abandoned the CD exchange. I was trying to limit the online chatting period because I kept creating a picture in my head of this smart, funny, adorable guy somewhere in Manhattan (or Jersey or even Philly if that's what it took) and then the actual date would always be a letdown. I was now going one step further and eliminating the pre-date phone call, because by Date #16 I could tell over the phone if a date was going to be bad, and even though the point was to go on seventeen *bad* dates, I'm telling you, *I hit a wall.*

That is how I ended up on a date with a guy I didn't realize had two hearing aids and a speech impediment. He had contacted me online (his picture was very cute), and when he asked if he could call to set up the date, rather than saying, "I tend to lose interest once I talk to someone on the phone," I just suggested we dispense with the pre-date bullshit and meet for coffee at such and such a place and time. That's when I realized maybe there is a point to the pre-date phone call, if only to clue you in to the possibility that your date might have a slight handicap, and that you might want to be prepared for it. You might want, for example, to pick a quieter restaurant. Of course you won't know if he *also* seems to produce an overabundance of saliva until you meet him in person. (If you are reading this, Man I Met for Coffee, I am sorry to sound so harsh. You were very nice, and I was weary from dating, and someone much nicer and more deserving than me has probably already fallen in love with you, and she, no doubt, is the reason you are reading this.)

I burned off my final bad date, Date #17, by accepting a second date with Date #11, and although he was even more bitter than ever, I was done! I was ready for my good date! Date #18. To celebrate this new optimistic phase of dating, I agreed to go to a singles party with a friend. A nice looking Italian dermatologist from Long Island gave me his card, and I also met a very cute money manager, and I decided to give him my card, but I accidentally handed him the dermatologist's card. (It's possible women are not cut out for dating this many people.)

In any case, the dermatologist called me and we proceeded to have the worst and strangest date I have ever experienced, making it clear that Benicio Del Toro must not have counted, because this had to be my seventeenth and final bad date. I couldn't withstand any more. Nobody could. A person needs at least one good date every eighteen dates in order to remain sane.

Bad Date #17 (formerly known as Good Date #18) was a half-hour late meeting me at Bar Code (his choice), which is a loud, many-leveled video arcade in the middle of Times Square. While I was waiting I tried a few games and discovered that it *is* actually possible to get a score of zero on the taxi simulator, which made me sympathize with New York cab drivers. But mostly I was feeling sorry for myself. When my date finally arrived he was angry about the parking and the traffic, then he took me directly to the Ferrari simulator so he could explain very loudly (so everyone around us could be impressed) how it was a good simulation, and he knew this because he actually owned and raced a Ferrari. Then this Ferrari-racing dermatologist took me to Mars 2112, which is a place you wouldn't know about unless you were a tourist with small children. The space shuttle ride was mercifully out of order, but unfortunately, I found out, we were there for dinner. If my date had displayed any sense of humor or irony, it might have been funny/silly, but he didn't and we actually sat in a black light–bathed, Styrofoam-walled bar, ordered from a laminated menu (never a good sign), and ate Intergalactic Chicken served by a Martian. I cannot explain why I made out with him, but I blame the "Martianis."

It was definitely a low point, and I think I was right about Benicio not counting because my next date, Date #18, was a very nice, very smart, very decent guy who'd lost his young wife to cancer two years prior. He'd spent an entire year mourning, even took off work to fully go through the grief, so I felt especially stupid when I was the one getting teary-eyed over my ex. This man, despite everything he'd been through, was ready for a new relationship and I, despite my seventeen bad dates, was not. That's when I realized there are no shortcuts, because it's not only time and distance you need after you lose a love, it's reflection.

That night I noticed I still had the roses my ex had sent in my bedroom (dried and displayed in a rare Martha Stewart moment), and I decided I didn't need them around anymore. I put them on the back of my bike and rode down to Battery Park City, where you can look out over the water to the Statue of Liberty, and I thought about all the people who came to America with practically nothing—people who had no idea what was in store for them, people who knew only that there was promise, and whatever the future held, it had to be better than what they were leaving behind. I wondered if maybe that's what I needed to do—have faith, and risk having nothing for a while. One by one I dropped the roses into the river and watched them float away.

it's not us . . . it's them

chapter nineteen

LAST CALL: A bachelor's final, desperate phone call warning ex-girlfriends and unrequited loves that he's about to go off the market, so act now!

It appears that even while speeding down the road to matrimony, some men are still scanning the horizon for an off-ramp. I'm talking about the "Last Call" phenomenon, and I feel I can call it a phenomenon because it happened to *three* of my female friends, and then it happened to me.

I received my Last Call recently when an ex I hadn't talked to for several years phoned to let me know he was getting married in a month, but he'd been dreaming about me four times a week. He wasn't going to tell his fiancée about the dreams, he explained, because she already feels he has some unresolved issues with me. (You think?) I basically responded with: "Well . . . congratulations on getting engaged," which seemed to throw him. I think he was hoping for something more along the lines of "That's so weird— I've been dreaming about you, too!" But I hadn't been dreaming about him, and frankly I was just happy one of my exes was getting married, because most of them have opted to travel indefinitely or join cults instead.

One woman I know received a Last Call from an ex the night before he got engaged, and she later discovered he'd called several exes that night, presumably to make sure there weren't any objections or better offers. Another heard from a male friend who's always had a crush on her—he just needed to make sure she wasn't interested in an experimental weekend fling before he got any more serious with his current girlfriend. And a third, Alyssa, got a call from a friend/ex-lover who basically wanted one Last Booty Call before succumbing to his girlfriend's pressure to get engaged, and in a moment of weakness, Alyssa agreed. (The ex didn't get engaged, by the way. Either he truly wasn't ready to commit or Alyssa is just *that* good.)

Last Call means the lights are flashing. It's closing time for the bachelor . . . time to order one last drink and look around to see who he wants to go home with for the Rest of His Life. These Last Calls might actually be a necessary part of the commitment process for men, like driving by the house you didn't buy one last time before signing the papers for the house you're buying. Maybe these are the good guys who choose a disease-free ex-girlfriend over a stripper from their bachelor party (she writes, desperately looking for an upside). The truth is, I'd hate to think the love of my life married me because somebody didn't have call waiting, but marriages are built on trust. Trust that the right people will end up together. Trust that true love can withstand any test. And trust that she'll simply say, "Well . . . congratulations on getting engaged."

chapter twenty

THE VISA DEFENSE: The claim, usually invoked by men, that "I paid, therefore I am innocent."

A man I know, an actor, recently spent four days in New York with a woman he freely admits was driving him crazy. He didn't admit this to her, of course, because that would be honest (and possibly hurtful), whereas pretending to have a great time offered many benefits. For example, it gave him the opportunity to brush up on his acting skills. It delayed their breakup until he was safely home in Los Angeles armed with bad cell phone connections and caller I.D. And most importantly, it didn't cut down on the sex. (Note: Nine out of ten times, when someone lies in a dating situation, I'd wager it's because the truth would cut down on the sex.) As he went on to detail the many things this woman did that annoyed him (including her inability to pick up on his that's-the-end-of-the-kiss signals), I couldn't help but feel sorry for her. I had glimpsed her future, and it didn't look pretty. After the inevitable petering out of phone calls, he would become just another unsolved dating mystery. "We had a perfect four days, then I never heard from him again," she would say to countless friends and strangers, all the while knowing less than I know, and I don't even know this guy so well. So I said as much. "It's not like you were forced to spend time with her, you *chose* to go to New York and visit." And to that he replied, "Hey, I paid for everything."

There it was—the Visa Defense. And he said it so earnestly, so simply, as if it were a baptism that cleansed him of his sins, or some kind of social "get out of jail free" card. On the contrary, paying for everything might have been his most deceptive act. In a world where men will sleep with women they don't like and wait three dates to kiss women they do, money becomes our only indicator of interest. Lately I'm not sure whether I'm on a date until the check arrives. If the guy throws down a credit card, I believe we might be embarking on more than a friendship. If he does it a second time, I at least assume I'm not "driving him crazy." A third time is very rare—he's either in love or he's expensing it.

I was once on a blind date that wasn't going so well, and when I offered to pay, the guy said, "Sure, you can kick some in." It was possibly the least romantic phrase ever uttered on a date, but it also paved the way for him not to call, and for me not to be disappointed. Not that I'm advocating payment (or partial payment) as a date-rating system. I'm simply saying to men that if you can't be honest, don't expect your credit card to buy you good will. Sure, I admit that four days of all-expenses-paid ignorance with a great-looking actor might be preferable to one night of annoyance with a cheap blind date, but in the event of heartbreak, money is rarely the loss a woman mourns.

chapter twenty-one

SLOPPY JOES: A new breed of men, spawned by technological advances, who are so busy dating they inadvertently call or e-mail the wrong women.

Men are getting sloppy. I don't know what's happening out there, but I've been getting a lot of secondhand sex. Which is not the same as sex. It's more like a wrong number.

Let me just preface this by saying that although I've been doing a lot of dating (or "research" as I like to call it when it goes badly), everyone I've gone out with over the past couple of months has deemed me a friend rather than a girlfriend.

One such "friend" recently left a message on my home machine sounding very flirty and saying, "Hey Cindy, good luck in the race on Sunday," and he went on to explain that the derivation of the word "news" is not, as some people believe, North East West South, but instead just the plural of new. He was later mortified to admit that he thought he was calling another Cindy.

Then another "friend" I met through an online dating service ("You *have* to try it! It's how I met my husband!" my friend Judy always insisted) sent me a long funny story that was going around the internet called "My Fake Job," and at the bottom he had accidentally included his entire online relationship with Alicia of Brooklyn. I'm talking everything from commenting on each other's dating profiles ("I would also like to learn to play canasta!") to exchanging *Planet of the Apes* reviews (she wonders if she should see the original again to appreciate the new one; he thinks the original was lacking as well) to a near deal-breaker (she likes Bon Jovi; he writes sarcastically, "Glad to know you're interested in the fine arts") to making their first date ("we can chat live if you like") to its tragic and inevitable conclusion—the sending of a funny online story called "My Fake Job." And all the while he's writing her the same flirty crap he wrote me not long ago, and she's all :-)s.

Perhaps technology—answering machines, BlackBerries, instant messaging, and e-mail—is the enemy we should fear. This might have been the point of *Planet of the Apes*, but I'm not sure because I didn't see it after reading Alicia's harsh review.

So there you have it. I'm not dating, but I'm in on a lot of other people's dates. The good "plural-of-new" is that second-hand sex often makes it clear you're better off being friends with these Sloppy Joes, because the second time around any guy's flirtations and come-ons seem a little stale.

chapter twenty-two

MALE FRIEND MORATORIUM: The decision, made by a single woman, that she doesn't need any more male friends; that from now on her answer to the question "Can we just be friends?" is "No."

I've noticed a disturbing trend among the single men I've met lately. When they say they just want to be friends, they *actually want to be friends*. It's not an annoying blow-off anymore; it's an annoying bona fide offer. They want to try that sushi restaurant I was raving about, exchange CDs and witty e-mails, hear singer/songwriters in groovy little clubs, hike, bike, play Ping-Pong, maybe even travel together. This would all be very exciting if there was a chance in hell of romance, but no, again, they "just want to be friends."

I know what you're thinking. They're gay, these men—they simply haven't come to terms with it yet! Sadly, repressed homosexuality only accounts for roughly half the men who don't want to date me. The other half have issues that are harder to pinpoint—issues like not knowing what they want to be when they grow up, not being over a previous girlfriend, not wanting to admit they prefer Asian women, or just plain not being attracted to me. But they all want to hang out.

"You're not a department store, you're a boutique," a male friend once advised. (He was an MBA, and this was before I declared my Male Friend Moratorium.) What he meant, I think, is that in the world of dating you're not trying attract *everyone*, you're trying to attract a very select group of people who are in the market for exactly what you're selling. So it's not necessarily a rejection when a man just wants to be friends. However, these new male friend wannabes are confusing because they appear to be in the market for what you're selling. They try the relationship on. They just don't buy.

I enacted my Male Friend Moratorium when I realized I was in a slump that consisted of meeting a cute guy, having one or two dinners with him, wondering why we weren't at least kissing goodnight, initiating that awkward conversation, finding out he's not really looking for a girlfriend, then feeling shamed into accepting his offer of friendship. I was never sure if these men genuinely wanted to be friends, thought they might grow to like me more over time, or hoped I'd eventually introduce them to Kristin Davis, but none of the above was great for the ego. Nevertheless, I accepted this social consolation prize because anyone who's faced the "Can we be friends?" question knows that saying you don't want to be friends is akin to saying, "It's too painful to be your friend. How can I be around you and not jump your bones?" And who wants to give a guy that satisfaction after he already rejected you . . . or, um, decided not to shop in your boutique?

I don't mean to imply that I don't enjoy and value male friends. I do. I've just reached capacity. And ultimately these new male friendships are not satisfying, because the more fun you have together, the more you wonder why your "friend" doesn't want to date you, and that can only lead to the kind of soul-searching best reserved for holidays home with your parents.

chapter twenty-three

SNOOZE-LOSE SYNDROME: The pressure single women face due to the miniscule amount of time a decent guy is actually available; our lamentable inability to put a guy on hold like a sweater.

The Snooze-Lose Syndrome is best illustrated with the quote: "She who hesitates is lost." I remember first understanding this frustrating phenomenon when I was looking for a house. House-hunting as a single woman is already slightly traumatic, because although it's a sign of career success to be able to buy a house alone, *you're buying a house ALONE! What's next? Seven cats? Are you throwing in the towel?* These were the thoughts in my head when, after exiting one particularly lovely house, my real estate agent told me we should make an offer NOW. On the car hood. Here's the paperwork. Well, I don't respond to pressure. I wanted to come back later with a friend . . . or fiancé. I didn't believe this house was going to "fly off the market" the very next day. Until it did. Actually, I think it was gone by nightfall. And now the same thing is happening in the dating world. It's a seller's market, and unfortunately, single men seem to be the sellers.

Here's why I know this to be true: Last year in New York a female friend fixed me up on a blind date with someone who, we realized during our pre-date phone call, also knew a male friend of mine. Curious for a second opinion, I asked my male friend his take on my prospective date, and he said, "Oh, that guy. Yeah, I don't know if that's gonna work out." Basically, he wasn't sure I'd think the guy was cute enough. "He's kind of a less good-looking Jeff Goldblum," he explained. It was hard to imagine, but true. My blind date was nice, funny, smart—but there was nothing happening for me in the chemistry department. I called my male friend the next day and told him he was right, no sparks, and then he did something a bit jarring. He said, "You know, if you're not interested, maybe I should fix him up with Elizabeth."

I know Elizabeth. Elizabeth has high standards. I started to panic. *He did take me to a nice restaurant. Maybe I should give him another chance. Maybe he could get his teeth fixed. Maybe I am shallow and unworthy of a relationship.* And while I was having these thoughts, he and Elizabeth went to dinner, fell in love, and moved in together. My male friend enjoys taking credit for fixing them up, but he only fixed them up after I reminded him this man existed. It was like I turned over a rock, found a single guy, and suddenly there was a feeding frenzy. I should note that I have seen Elizabeth out with this man, and they are terribly happy, and he looks cuter than I remembered, which is always the case once a guy is in a relationship.

Another friend, Laurie, recently heard that a handsome, successful man she knew was separating from his wife, so she called him the day of the news to ask him to a charity event. He accepted the date, and hours later she found out he was gay, which was why he was separating from his wife, and that he was involved with his male assistant. Her story is the essence of the Snooze-Lose Syndrome, because it illustrates just how tiny a decent guy's window of availability is. The time between which this man was officially married and officially gay was about three-and-a-half minutes, at which point he was officially unavailable to women AND men. You snooze, you lose, baby. Of course, the danger is feeling like dating is a game of musical chairs, and you better grab a seat—any seat—quick. *But I don't respond to pressure. I think there's someone out there who is right for me, and* . . . Okay, who just grabbed the last chair?

it's not us . . . it's the city

SPORTS DATES: A seemingly "fun" alternative to dinner and a movie, usually involving a little healthy competition, which is not always healthy for a new relationship.

For me, the worst part of living in southern California is not the danger of riots, fires, mudslides, earthquakes, or the arrival of killer bees—it's the weather. When it's sunny and warm every day of the year, it's virtually impossible to get a relationship off the ground without eventually going on a "sports date."

I'm not talking about a "professional sporting event date" (which is the way men get back at us for dragging them to all those crafts fairs and antiques shops), because regardless how fervently you cheer or how far you have to walk for a hot dog, attending a sporting event is basically passive.

A genuine sports date pits you and your love interest against each other in a competitive activity. This might take the form of tennis, golf, volleyball, hiking, biking, skiing, white-water rafting, blading or, if you live in southern California, all of the above in a twenty-four-hour period.

"Wait a minute," you say, "hiking isn't competitive." This is the kind of naiveté that gets women into trouble. Remember, men are taught from childhood to compete at everything. If your date is torn between wanting to beat you or bond with you, chances are his competitive indoctrination will win out (which is why my friend Alyssa, when playing Monopoly with her boyfriend, had to take her money with her when she got up to go to the bathroom).

Sports dates do have a certain appeal. Women, in fact, are often the first to suggest them. But before you blithely enter the world of shared sports activity, here's a list of mental kneepads to help you survive and learn from the experience.

Do not engage in a sport that either of you played at varsity level in high school or college. I learned this the hard way when I suggested tennis to a guy who'd been playing since he was seven. Although our first two dates had gone quite well, at some point during that tennis match he began to hate me. He not only tried to kill me with a couple of serves, he actually told me to "hustle." That's when I started to hate him back. No one is entitled to use the term "hustle" unless he or she is in an official coaching capacity. Nor should you offer your date any unsolicited pointers. It may bridge the skill gap, but it will inevitably widen the emotional one.

Try not to get carried away. Some women are suckers for proving themselves in front of men. Case in point: An old boyfriend and I rented Boogie boards during a trip to Hawaii, but everywhere we went, I thought the water looked too rough. Then he threw out what I perceived to be a challenge: "You never know if the water is too rough until you've been in it." Within minutes we were kicking out to sea, despite a five-foot swell, a serious undertow and the curious absence of other swimmers. As an experienced surfer paddled out to rescue us, I remember thinking two things: a) Never let your I'll-show-him spirit get in the way of common sense, and b) People on the beach look really, really small from out here.

Try to choose a sport that involves rental equipment. That way, whoever loses or gets tired first has something other than skill to blame. "I never had this problem with my Rollerblades. The wheels on these rentals are really bad."

Avoid the temptation to gloat if you beat him at his own game. My dental hygienist once went bowling with her boyfriend, who plays every week in a league, and "kicked his butt." Afterward, she gleefully announced the victory over the bowling alley loud-speaker. This, she admits in retrospect, was not a good idea. During the silent car ride home, she felt like a loser as well.

Be aware that some sports dates are compatibility tests. And you both might fail. My friend Pamela spent a disastrous weekend with a boyfriend who invited her to go white-water rafting. Since he'd been a river rafting guide, she thought he'd be patient, encouraging, and laid back. Wrong. He scowled at her when she pulled her wet suit on inside out, yelled when she dented a tent pole, and when she lost a paddle in the rapids, he suggested she jump in after it. By the time she got sunscreen in her eyes ("Any idiot knows you don't put it on your forehead!"), the relationship was over.

You always have the option of saying, "I'd like to, but I'm al-phabetizing my CDs." A guy recently invited me to join him and his friends in a game of paintball. This is a war-simulation game where players fire paint-filled bullets at each other. "Actually," he elaborated, "we don't give the women guns. We let them be hostages, though. We tie you to a tree, and if the other team gets too close, we shoot you." Oddly enough, I was busy.

chapter twenty-five

GOING HOLLYWOOD: The process of transforming from a nice Midwestern girl-next-door into someone who has a psychic, trainer, masseuse, agent, and nutritionist on her speed dial.

I realized I'd gone Hollywood when I called my therapist from my car phone to tell her I'd be late due to traffic, but it wasn't due to traffic. It was due to the fact that a psychic in the Hollywood Hills had a last-minute opening, and I needed to know if I was going to marry my boyfriend. (I couldn't tell my therapist that. I don't want her to think I'm crazy!) The good news is I haven't *completely* gone Hollywood. For example, I don't see the personal trainer whose name is Name. I still have nothing to add when the lunch conversation turns to why used jets are a better value than new. And I will not, as a fellow television writer did, hire someone to teach my kid to ride a bike.

Still, too many nonfat mocha Frappuccinos *no whipped cream* have been brought to me by an unpaid intern. Too many friends have suggested an annual appointment with the Vedic astrologer, Chakrapani. Too often I have vetoed a date because of his television credits. Last week I was in a meeting where a producer said, "*E.R.* in space? Is it a TV show? No-brainer!" and as I followed his gaze to a pinned-up sketch of an intergalactic hospital, instead of laughing, I acted impressed.

I tried to trace how this happened—how I became blasé about seeing Arnold Schwarzenegger on the bike path—and I discovered, perhaps not surprisingly, the stages of going Hollywood correspond exactly with the five stages of dealing with death.

Stage One: Denial and Isolation

It is not uncommon, upon moving from a nice little town in the Midwest, where there are seasons and size 12 women, to a sprawling city like Los Angeles, where there are riots and earthquakes and go-go boots, for a person to feel lost and alone—as if the world is closing in on you, squashing you into a little metal box, when in reality you're just stuck in traffic behind a bunch of other shell-shocked Midwesterners waiting for a left turn arrow that doesn't exist.

One way of dealing with this adjustment is denial. Pretend it's only temporary. You're just checking things out. You'll give it a year and see what happens. This stage is marked by a lack of furniture in your apartment. Sometimes by the lack of an apartment. Note: In Hollywood people without apartments are not homeless, they are house-sitters.

Stage Two: Anger

As you learn what it takes to survive in Hollywood you will feel a certain amount of anger. Why do I need an agent? Who put passion fruit in my iced tea? How thin do you have to be to go to the gym? Why don't the appliances come with the apartment? Why is there no market for a non-commercial screenplay about an alien love triangle? Why did the guy at the frame shop ask if I wanted bulletproof glass? Where are the straight men? When *is* rush hour?

This is a necessary, if unpleasant stage. This is a stage when a mentor would be helpful, but chances are you will scare yours off. This is the stage during which many people become bad stand-up comics.

Stage Three: Bargaining

Once you've worn a sweater in seventy-degree weather, leaving Los Angeles is no longer an option. You now have to make this work, which means rationalizing participation in everything you've been making fun of.

You will write or act or film something "commercial," but vow that your next project will be from the heart. You will buy a car phone, but only for emergencies and maybe an occasional call during off-peak hours. You will see a psychic, but just for kicks (mine had a diploma on her wall from my alma mater, Northwestern) and from that point on, you will only date "men with the initials J, G, or R." You will rent Rollerblades, but you won't learn how to stop. You will valet park, but only because you were running late. You will take a scenic hike from the top of Paseo Miramar and marvel at the smog, which you will start calling "hazy sunshine."

Stage Four: Depression

This stage usually occurs around the holidays, specifically holidays you have to work through. It is often occasioned by the sight of people buying Christmas trees in shorts, or the specter of that giant menorah on Santa Monica Boulevard, which is annoying even if you're Jewish. Especially if you're Jewish. You will miss the snow, your friends, your family, those wide open spaces in which you used to park. You'll wonder if it's all worth it, whether you're starting to watch the credits more closely than the movie, whether being a player means being married three or four times and getting addicted to something and going to a twelve-step program and finding true love in a yoga class. You will try to express this to an L.A. friend who will say, "You know, that would make a great movie." This, more than any other phrase, is what will drive you to a therapist.

Stage Five: Acceptance

When your commercial project is a box-office hit, it will slowly dawn on you that perhaps your non-commercial ideas are non-commercial because they stink. You will start using your car phone all the time, simply because you can't wait five minutes to get home and get your messages, or because you want your grilled veggie pizza to arrive at the same time you do. You will accept that D-e-b-b-e-e is a legitimate spelling, even for a man. You will unapologetically toss around terms like *my interior designer*, *my masseuse*, and *my herbalist*. You will finally admit that you live in L.A.—even to your car insurance agent. You will start considering private school for your kids, even though you always preferred the diversity of public school, even though you don't have kids or any real prospects for a relationship—initials J, G, R, or otherwise.

The trunk of your car will be home to hiking boots, a tennis racket, two spec scripts and an earthquake survival kit. Your agent (you gave up on tooting your own horn after you alienated several friends) will get you a job on a television show that only your parents will watch. Some nights you will work until 3 A.M. and leave tired and jumpy from M&M's, swearing never again to order the Chinese chicken salad from Jerry's Deli. Then you'll notice a handsome P.A. on a bike, silhouetted by the light of an open sound stage, and you'll hear the hammering and sawing of a set being built, and as you walk to your very own parking space, you'll realize that somehow, despite everything, you've grown to like it here. And as that thought warms and frightens you, you'll drive out the historic studio gates and onto the 405 freeway, where, amazingly, there will be a traffic jam.

chapter twenty-six

RELOCATIONSHIPS: The kind of relationship that necessitates moving to a place where you would never consider living, but you *must* now consider it because there's a decent single guy there (or rumors of a decent single guy).

Greetings from the Bad Hair State! I am in Florida for the month of September (coincidentally Back-to-School month) relearning how to play the role of *girlfriend*, which in Boca seems to imply acrylic nails, breast implants, and tennis skirts. However, it is Hurricane Season (something nobody adequately explained to me) so the heat, humidity, and daily downpours have made a mockery of my hair products, rental convertible, and optimism.

In an effort to fit in, I am working out with a personal trainer three days a week, and I am happy to announce that I have already lost . . . my dignity. I realized this when, for the first two weeks, my trainer never once asked what I did for a living. I went from being impressed that she didn't care, to annoyed, to a state of dropping obvious hints—like that I was going to the Emmys and I still hadn't found shoes to match my gown and it was my boyfriend's *first time*. Finally in the middle of some chest presses I blurted out that I WRITE FOR *SEX AND THE CITY*, making it abundantly clear that even if I say I'm tired of talking about what I do, I am completely lost when I can't talk about what I do. (Evidently many women in Boca are not required to do much more than look fabulous. They are *capable* of doing more, and many *do* work, but for the most part the typical Boca Babe's life seems to be about country clubs, couture, and kids.) Which brings me to my "be careful what you wish for" story.

After spending the last decade worrying when and *if* I'm ever going to have children, I suddenly found myself in the back of an SUV with three of them. One was my boyfriend's five-year-old daughter who always dresses better than I do. The other two belonged to the couple we were traveling with (an ex–Navy SEAL and his extremely fit wife and her extraordinary new boobs). Their son was potty training, I found out, when he announced from the car seat next to me, "Mommy, I'm going pee pee," and we immediately had to pull to the side of the road and stick him out the window, but apparently we didn't do this fast enough.

· I have to add that this family was late meeting us in the Office Depot parking lot where we were consolidating into one car (another thing I was not adequately prepared for) because on the way, they witnessed an old woman driving off the road, and the Navy SEAL dove into a canal and pulled her out of her sinking car but couldn't save her. Thus their kids, every once in a while, would say things like, "Daddy tried to help the lady but she's in heaven," and "We saw the lady with her shirt *and bra* off." Maybe I was the only one who heard them, (this is entirely possible because I noticed that parents acquire the ability to carry on a normal conversation amid complete chaos, whereas non-parents still hear everything except what is being said by the other adults), but in any case, I seemed to be the only one worried these kids might be a bit traumatized.

This was all in an effort to get to Billie Swamp Safari to see alligators, which we did, and once we were on the airboat (which only lasted twenty minutes and took an hour and a half and two Advil purchased from the gift shop to get to), my boyfriend's daughter started crying hysterically and saying, "I want to get off! I want to get off!" Luckily the airboat's fan is very noisy—you are required to wear earplugs anyhow—so I was able to enjoy the ride even sitting next to a screaming little girl. It was kind of surreal actually. Her mouth was open and tears were streaming down her face, but you couldn't hear a thing, and if you looked in the other direction out to the swampy Everglades, it really didn't hinder the experience at all. Thus making me think an airboat is the way to get around once you have kids. Or should I say *if* you have kids, I thought to myself during the ride home as large plastic bow-and-arrow souvenirs were unwrapped and somehow deemed a suitable car game. Maybe it was the heat, maybe it was the fried gator bites I ate for lunch, but suddenly I realized that for a brief Boca moment, I was enjoying the *if*.

chapter twenty-seven

THE *REAL* NEW YORK MARATHON: The inspiring, embarrassing, and sometimes debilitating things you must endure in order to live and love in Manhattan.

Lily Tomlin says New York is always knowing where your purse is. I have a few definitions to add to the list.

New York is being certain that it is just a matter of time before you run into your boyfriend's ex-girlfriend, even though this is a city of more than eight million, because her favorite bar is the piano bar below your apartment and she belongs to your health club. She is not beautiful, his friends reassure you, but you might say she is exotic.

New York is overhearing phrases such as Aesthetically Pleasing and Incredibly Powerful.

New York is watching Wesley, Austin, and Lacey Goldstein grow into their names. And learning from your friend's daughter that chartreuse was strictly last season.

New York is seeing the best and worst comedy in the world, and when it is bad, you leave feeling like you collectively flopped as an audience and perhaps you were having an off night.

New York is having a discussion with the homeless man who lives outside your apartment and telling him, "Eddie, I need to sleep," and him telling you he understands but needs to make a living and if he has to sing outside a piano bar then that's what he has to do. And even though you took Theories of Argumentation at a prestigious university while he took drugs in Washington Square Park, you lie awake in bed and he continues to sing "Ain't Too Proud to Beg" outside your window.

New York is learning the hard way that on opening night when a woman races across the room to ask *whose* dress you're wearing, she is not asking from whom it was borrowed, but for the name of the designer. New York is understanding why, every once in a while, a very high-powered executive thinks back nostalgically on the modest house where she grew up and realizes that she lived in the Taj Mahal and didn't even know it. And defining success as the luxury of reading a menu from left to right.

New York is having to decide if you want to sleep with your date while the cab is waiting, and feeling judged by the driver, and in the morning feeling judged by your doorman.

New York is one huge impending deadline and a barrage of new assignments, and if there is anyplace that will make you feel guilty for not getting around to something, it's New York.

New York is participating in the giant, clumsy ballet of Grand Central, where you run, run, run for the shuttle and make it just as the doors are closing, and there is a slight letdown when nobody even high-fives you. New York is that one person, still sitting on the shuttle, wondering if this is the right stop.

New York is riding the subway and having the beggars practice one-upmanship. *I am a Vietnam vet. I am a Vietnam vet and I have no arm. I am a Vietnam vet and I have no arm and I have three children in need of diapers. I am not a mean man. I just look dangerous. This gun is not loaded.*

New York is seeing Madonna jogging and realizing she jogs and you jog and perhaps all that separates you is the fact that you prefer to wear your underwear underneath. And living next door to Ethan Hawke and seeing him only when you look like the cleaning lady. And not speaking to your roommate for three days because he refused Ethan Hawke's package that was sent to your apartment by mistake.

New York is a transvestite throwing a lit cigarette in a homeless woman's bag, and even though you quietly remove the cigarette before she goes up in flames, your boyfriend feels compelled to tell the transvestite and his eight friends that they *really* have *a lot* of class. And as they follow you to your door, Eddie the homeless man asks if you need any help.

New York is the irony of reading the finest literature in the world and speaking only of the weather. It is building an entire wardrobe of black.

New York is having your friend, the struggling actor, run over out of breath to tell you that he was finally cast as Gorilla Number 1, which entails walking onstage, pissing on a statue, and leaving.

New York is discovering that a cat is a legitimate pet even though you once swore you would never own one. And naming your mouse after someone you despise so you can eventually kill it. And watching a roach take shelter from your jet stream of Raid by dodging into a nearby Roach Motel. And empathizing.

okay, maybe some of it's us

ROCK BOTTOM: A low point, typically thought to require drugs or alcohol, but also achievable by singles who have "tried to be open-minded," a.k.a. "lowered their standards" to the point of almost no return.

The phone rings and wakes me. It's 6:15 A.M. Sunday morning in New York. Who would call at 6:15, I wonder? Maybe Rob, the married guy I've been seeing in Portland. I know you're not supposed to see married guys, by the way. I'm not proud of the fact that I was seeing a married guy. The thing is, every single woman, if she's single long enough, ends up in a relationship with a married guy. This includes men who don't tell you they're married when you meet them, men who tell you they're getting divorced, men who never plan to get divorced—and in most cases, all three wrapped up in a handsome little package.

Now, women, God love them, have the amazing ability to believe these relationships might somehow work out, even though we are hard-pressed to find examples of this kind of thing working out, and we are bombarded (by friends and Dear Abby columns) with examples of this kind of thing *not* working out. Still, every woman who has ever dated a married guy has believed that she is different. That this is love. That this was meant to be, and the timing was just off by a few years and possibly some kids. You see, for single women, the fairy tale is ever evolving, and when you think you're in love, you can figure out a way to make the fairy tale include a married guy. It's part of our charm and part of our downfall.

Of course, my "affair" if it must be called that (I would prefer to call it my "derailment") ended exactly the way these things are supposed to end, with Rob realizing how much he loved and cherished his family, and me realizing that even though you go through life thinking you are in your own movie, occasionally you realize you've stumbled into someone else's movie, and you are not, in fact, Julia Roberts. At best you're one of the Arquette sisters—in for an act or two, a catalyst for someone else's story. Things will not necessarily end happily for you. Your character may not even learn a lesson.

But the morning the phone woke me I was drowsy and deluded, and I still thought I was Julia Roberts.

The phone rings again. *How can it be Rob? It's only 3:15 in Portland.*

Me: Hello?

Rob: I can't sleep. *He sounds weird, troubled.*

Me: Is something wrong?

Rob: What are you doing?

Me: Talking to you.

Rob: What are you wearing?

Me: Flannel pajamas. *I laugh.* Not very sexy, huh? What are you wearing?

Rob: A shirt and nothing else. Take off the bottoms.

Me: Really?

Rob: Yeah.

Me: . . . Okay. *I'm thinking about how I recently told Rob, when he was feeling like a creepy guy for falling for someone while he was married, that he wasn't a creepy guy, that creepy guys drive flashy sports cars and buy their girlfriends lingerie and have phone sex. Is that why he's doing this—because he's feeling like he made his creepy bed, he might as well lie in it?*

Rob: Unbutton the top.

Me: . . . Okay.

Him: Now show me your lips.

Me: *I briefly think, He wants me to smile? Oh, THOSE lips. This is weird. Rob doesn't talk like that, although we've never had phone sex before. Maybe he's trying to be kinky, and he's just not very good at it.*

Him: Tell me to lick your pussy.

Me: (weakly) Lick my pussy. *Wait a minute! What if this isn't Rob?*

Him: Now what do you want me to do?

Me: *I could be talking to a stranger! A weirdo! I should hang up! But what if it is Rob trying to be sexy and I hang up on him? Maybe I should say, "Who is this?" No, because if it IS Rob, won't he think that's odd since I was already playing along? My solution is to laugh and say* . . . Hey, Rob, how do I know this is you?

Him: (pause) It's me.

Me: *Despite the early hour, I come up with this:* What T-shirt do I have of yours?

Him: (long pause) The black one.

Me: *That's right! But it could have been a lucky guess.* What does it say?

Him: You tell me.

Me: No, you tell me.

Him: (long pause) How do you like my big hard cock!

That is not what the T-shirt says. I hang up. I call Rob's cell, hoping it was him, hoping we'll laugh about how I thought it could have been anybody else. He doesn't answer. Of course he doesn't answer! It's 3:15 there! He *and his wife* are asleep! A glimmer of hope—maybe he was drunk! Which would be bad, because he's a recovered alcoholic, but it still seems better than the alternative— that I just took off my flannel pajamas, even apologized they weren't *sexier*, and said "Lick my pussy" for some New York wacko I thought was my married boyfriend!!! I hope he'll call back. That ROB will call back. No one calls. Not Rob. Not the wacko.

You'd think at least the wacko would call back. I was certainly a good sport. I am at once mortified and insulted. I look up at the ceiling. I look up at rock bottom.

chapter twenty-nine

DATER'S REMORSE: That sick feeling you get after dating someone you didn't really need and couldn't emotionally afford.

I never imagined this would happen, but three men are fighting over me. They call me repeatedly. They ply me with gifts. They beg me for a commitment. Yes, they're just AT&T, MCI, and Sprint salesmen interested in being my long-distance carrier, but what I'm relishing—aside from the attention—is the sense that I am in complete control.

In fact, just the other day my ex (phone carrier, that is) called to find out what went wrong. Had I been unhappy? What would it take to win me back? Turns out all it took was two thousand frequent flier miles. I switched, just like that. I didn't worry about how my current carrier would feel, or how it might affect my Friends and Family. Now if only I could use that kind of healthy judgment when it comes to my love life.

The unfortunate truth is that while most of us are savvy shoppers, we're not sufficiently selective when looking for relationships, and that's why we often suffer from dater's remorse.

Perhaps we should try to apply conventional consumer wisdom to men as well as merchandise. How satisfying love might be if we always remembered to:

Go with a classic, not a trend. We all know it's unwise to spend a week's salary on vinyl hip-huggers. But when it comes to men, even the most conservative among us occasionally invests in the human equivalent of a fashion fad. The furthest I ever strayed from a classic was during college. I wrote a paper about the Guardian Angels, those street toughs who unofficially patrol inner-city neighborhoods, and being a very thorough student, I ended up dating one. He wore a red beret and entertained me by demonstrating martial arts moves in my dorm room. I remember telling my concerned roommate how he was *sooo* much more interesting than those boring MBA types everybody else was dating. Of course, what initially seemed like a fun, impulse buy turned out to require more of an emotional investment than I was willing to make. It took me two months to break up with him—two months of getting persistent late-night calls, angry letters, and unannounced visits to my dorm room door, which I envisioned him kicking down someday. The good thing about MBAs: They're familiar with the expression "Cut your losses."

Beware of the phrase "Some assembly required." Anyone who has tried to follow translated-from-Swedish directions for putting together a swivel chair understands that when you've got to assemble something yourself, the money you save isn't worth the time you spend. The same goes for men. Many women think that even though a guy is not exactly "together," we can easily straighten him out. The fact is that fixer-uppers are more likely to stay forever flawed, no matter what we do. My friend Jenny fell for a forty-one-year-old bachelor, despite the fact that he spent their first few dates detailing his dysfunctional family and boasting that he went to the same shrink as the Menendez brothers. "Six weeks later, when he announced he couldn't handle a relationship, it shouldn't have surprised me," says Jenny, who now looks for men requiring a little less duct tape.

Make sure your purchase goes with the other things you own. I once fell in love with a very expensive purple velvet couch, and I seriously considered buying it, even though it would mean getting my cat declawed, and I had signed an agreement when I adopted her that I would never do that. But the couch . . . the couch . . . I visited it a few more times, but I didn't buy, and not just out of sympathy for my cat. I realized that if I owned that couch, I'd have to replace all my comfy, old stuff with new furniture equal in quality and style to the purple couch. Men can be like that, too. You're drawn to them because they're attractively different, but being with them may mean changing your entire life. For example, while dating a long-distance bicyclist, my friend Janet found herself suddenly following his training regimen: bowing out of social events just as the fun began, rising at an hour at which she normally went to bed, and replacing fine dining with intensive carbo-loading. And the only bike she ever rode was the stationary one at the gym.

Check with previous owners. Once beyond age twenty-five, most men would have to be classified as secondhand, and we all know how risky it is to buy used merchandise. Therefore, it's up to you to do some basic consumer research. Find out how many previous owners your selection has had. If he's such a steal, why is he still on the lot? Is it because his exterior is a bit unsightly, or because he's fundamentally a lemon? (Before becoming too critical, bear in mind that *you* are still on the lot.)

Caveat emptor. Following these guidelines won't guarantee a great relationship, but it will help you cut down on the number of times you feel dater's remorse. Obviously looking for a husband is a bit more complicated than choosing a major appliance, but since there are no lifetime guarantees or lemon laws for men, it pays to be a savvy shopper.

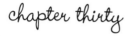

DO NOT RESUSCITATE ROMANCE (DNRR) ORDER: A directive that you are not, under any circumstances, allowed to revive or "restart the heart" of a past relationship.

Valentine's Day is a difficult time for singles. It's a time when, faced with the prospect of ordering Chinese for one, you might start missing a past love and wondering what it would be like to just "hang out together." That's how I found myself sleeping with a guy I'd spent a year trying to get over, someone I know I have no future with, who has told me we have no future. And yet, I somehow managed to get upset when I realized we *still* had no future, and that's when my friend Kate issued a DNRR. (Note: It's perfectly legal for a caring friend or family member to issue a DNRR if you prove to be incapable of doing so yourself, which apparently I was.) "You are not allowed to see him anymore," Kate said firmly. "You have to let this one die."

You basically know when you need to pull the plug, when any other action will lead to more pain and a further loss of dignity, but a DNRR is easier issued than executed. Therefore I was supposed to call Kate whenever I felt the urge to resuscitate, a strategy which worked until the night I called and she had a guy there, making it clear that my messed-up love life was now messing up other people's love lives. So we came up with a supplemental DNRR strategy: the Pretzel Plan.

The Pretzel Plan, like so many great innovations throughout history, evolved quite by accident when I took my sports car in for a tune-up and they gave me an SUV loaner. As soon as I got behind the wheel of this mammoth machine I felt the urge to do something I couldn't do in my little sports car, like have two kids and drive them to soccer practice. But I only had the car for a day, so Kate and I decided I should go to Costco and get some huge product, like twenty-four rolls of Bounty, and then I wouldn't call or e-mail my guy until it was gone. So that's what I did. I went to Costco for the first time ever to buy something huge—heartbreak huge—and I was wandering around this giant warehouse with this giant cart thinking I need something bigger than that eight-pound jar of spaghetti sauce, and I finally settled on a giant container of Dutch pretzels. And I don't really like pretzels, which was part of the appeal. The beauty of this plan is that it gives you a big visual reminder that relationships take time (and pretzels) to get over, and you shouldn't revive one just because it's a holiday.

In fact, your true Valentine might be a friend with a heart bigger than anything at Costco, who loves you enough to know when it's time to issue a DNRR.

chapter thirty-one

THE FREQUENT CRIER CONUNDRUM: Men
who are too sensitive and the women who can't love them.

You know how men are always saying that you don't need makeup, you look better without it? So one day, what the hell, you leave your lashes undefined, and every man in the office asks if you're feeling all right, you look so . . . tired. Well, women have their own sucker line: We tell men it's okay to cry. We tell them they can do it anytime and we will be standing by with Kleenex and sympathy. Lots of men are still wary, but others are opening up those ducts—only to learn the hard way that women haven't exactly worked out the details.

Admittedly, almost all women find it a touching, even exciting moment of vulnerability the very first time a normally stoic man cries. But what about the next time, and the next? The truth is, many of us would agree with my friend Susan, who says, "I like a man who's not afraid to cry . . . but doesn't." Ask yourself: If a man you were dating cried on a semiregular basis—say, he indulged in one good cry for every ten of yours—could you handle it?

Gaby thought she could. She was dating a man whose sensitivity was the initial attraction: He expressed emotion, showed compassion, responded openly to her questions. When he shed a few tears in conversations about the way his life was going, she was flattered that he would reveal so much to her. Then one pivotal night he completely broke down. We're talking three hankies, convulsive shaking, that attractive state of trying to speak while gasping for air. Gaby abruptly ran out of compassion: "On the outside I was supportive," she says, "but on the inside I was thinking, *Just pull it together*." Soon after, she broke off the relationship.

The question, according to Los Angeles psychotherapist Toby Salter, is this: "You say you want a feeling man, but do you have the strength to deal with a feeling man?" Salter says there's a real gap between the level of sensitivity we say we want and the level we're able to handle: "Women are not quite the Olympian intimacy machines we pretend to be." One problem is lack of experience; because we haven't seen men cry much in the past, their tears alarm us. Has some tragedy occurred, we wonder; is he cracking up?

Here's where women who grew up with emotionally expressive fathers have a leg up on the rest of us. My friend Cathy says her father, a scientist, "was very matter-of-fact most of the time, but he'd get teary over certain things—a well chosen Christmas present, a heartfelt card, a piece of poetry. Seeing him cry made me feel closer to him." And it helped prepare her for her husband's emotionalism after the arrival of their baby. "Bruce will get tears in his eyes when he's holding the baby and talking about all the little adventures they're going to have," she says. "I get teary-eyed just thinking about it."

I get teary-eyed just typing it.

Which brings us to another factor that can affect your tolerance for tears: Are you a frequent crier yourself? My friend Kristy definitely falls into that category, and she both tolerates and appreciates a man who cries occasionally too. "If a man absolutely never cries, that's a red flag to me," she says. "I wonder, do you think it's inappropriate to cry? Because if you do, you're going to hate me."

Not all frequent criers are seeking same, however. Rosie, who watches Hallmark Hall of Fame presentations just for the commercials ("A good cry every fifteen minutes!"), admits she feels uncomfortable when she sees a man crying. "Maybe I'm old-fashioned," she says.

Or maybe she has a double standard. If so, she's not alone. Gaby would never put a limit on the number of breakdowns I'm allowed, but she granted her boyfriend only a few tearful episodes before ditching him. Where women are concerned, we consider no crisis too small, no movie-of-the-week too hokey, to justify tears. And if we run out of reasons to cry, PMS gives us carte blanche.

The rules for men are much more complicated. While we may adore a man who tears up at weddings, breaks down at a friend's funeral, or cries at the birth of his baby, we're likely to panic if he sobs over finances or troubles at work. I heard about a couple whose apartment was robbed, and almost more disturbing than the robbery was the woman's discovery of her boyfriend sitting alone, crying at the kitchen table. It was a time when she needed him to be strong, but he was feeling just as violated and frightened as she was. The message to men is clear: You can cry out of feelings of happiness and sadness, but not out of fear, frustration, or weakness. We know you feel those emotions, but would you mind repressing them?

Women have been given a similar dictum on anger. We feel angry, but we're taught that it's unattractive and unfeminine to express it. The end result is that women get sick because they're repressing anger and men get angry because they're repressing fear. This raises the question: Does equality between the sexes mean we have to be equally miserable?

The answer, of course, is no. But men and women do have to give each other more emotional leeway—to rant and rave when we're angry, to cry when we're feeling vulnerable. If we really want men to share their most intimate hopes and dreams and fears, we'd better be willing to share the Kleenex.

chapter thirty-two

EGGSISTENTIAL CRISIS: A panic attack, common among women in their late thirties, which is triggered by the realization that your desire to have children and your desire not to settle might be mutually exclusive.

You get what you get. That's what a married friend told me recently, because that's what a married friend told her years ago when she was still single and rattling off her checklist of the things she wanted in a man. At the time, it struck her as a depressing statement, a thinly veiled endorsement of lowering your standards, but now that she's married, she says, it's true. You get what you get.

She told me this, I think, because I was musing that although I am very happy in my current relationship, I'm not sure it's "enough." I'm not sure he makes me the best version of me. (Incidentally, in my continuing quest to figure out the formula for the "right" relationship, the question "Does he make me the best version of me?" has replaced the checklist as my most useful dating tool. I feel good about that, although I wonder if the next step is replacing the "best version of me" question with the question: "Does the sperm donor have a history of drugs?") My point is—I no longer have time for these thoughts. At thirty-seven, I am acutely aware that my friends and family are gently but effectively telling me I need to shut up and marry my boyfriend or break up and find somebody else quick.

That's the essence of dating in your thirties. There is no time to ruminate. Every move could mean the difference between becoming part of a traditional family and becoming a woman who wears caftans, travels to exotic places alone, and brings back elephant tusks for her nephews.

Dating in your thirties means constantly debating whether you're picky in a good way or picky in a bad way, and whether being selfish is an accomplishment or a detriment. This is why I find myself longing for my twenties, a time when you could simply *be* in a relationship. We didn't worry about whether love would last forever. We worried about fruit as a source of carbs. It seemed like we had all the time in the world. I even recall thinking dating was "fun." We knew love would happen eventually. We just didn't know how many dates and diets and disasters "eventually" could entail.

I would like to state, for the record, that I still believe there's a great love out there for each and every one of us. I feel completely confident that none of my amazing single friends will end up alone, and they feel confident I won't either. None of us, however, feel confident that our knights in shining armor understand the friggin' time pressure we're under.

In an effort to ease this pressure, I have, at various points in my life, tried to make peace with the concept of adopting, freezing my eggs, or having a baby with a gay or platonic friend. On a bad day these seem like various forms of waving the white flag; on a good day they seem like empowering solutions, ways of taking matters into my own hands, controlling the things I can and assuring that I will get everything I want, just not in the usual order.

I have a friend who recently adopted a child as a single mother because she got tired of waiting for all the pieces to fall into place. Now she has a beautiful little daughter from China *and* she's dating more than ever. We've talked about why this might be—why she is suddenly so popular with the opposite sex (especially since her fear was that telling a man she had a child would be like telling him she had herpes), and we came up with two theories: 1) She was always a very successful, independent, and self-sufficient woman, so maybe before men saw her as intimidating, and now they see a single mother and a fatherless child and they understand how they fit into her life. Or 2) It might be simpler than that. It might just be that she's happy. She doesn't have the pressure of a biological clock anymore, and men probably sense that, so they can relax, and she can date like she's in her twenties again.

Although my friend is an inspiring reminder that sometimes the revised fairy tale is even better than the original, I'm not sure what the solution will be for me. I do know that I don't want to settle just to win this race against my viable eggs, but I also don't want to be unrealistic and wait indefinitely for perfection if it's true that in love and STDs, you get what you get.

your new boyfriend

CLOSE-TROPHOBIA: A heightened state of anxiety and agitation occurring when a person who's been single for a prolonged period of time tries to let another person into his/her life and apartment.

I became aware I was close-trophobic when I found myself in a long-distance relationship, and the problem wasn't the distance, it was the lack of it during our weekends together. This patient and kind man would travel five hours by train to see me in New York, and all I had to do was share my apartment, which is not teeny tiny like most New York apartments. It only *felt* teeny tiny to me when there was a man in it for forty-eight hours. This panicked sense that "two's a crowd" is often the first sign that you've become close-trophobic.

Now, possibly—*hopefully*—this man was simply not the one for me, and when the right man comes along I will welcome him with open arms and open doors. However, it's also possible that, like many successful thirty-something singles, my years of living alone have made me the relationship equivalent of Rain Man. Why else, when faced with a handsome houseguest, would I be thinking things like: " 'Course . . .'course it's eleven minutes to *Sopranos* and spin class is in the morning and this is *not* my side of the bed. *Definitely* not my side of the bed."

Although asking your parents to stay in a hotel when they visit is generally considered "progress," asking a boyfriend to stay in a hotel is generally considered "cuckoo." Therefore the close-trophobe has no choice but to suffer through this uncomfortable period or suffer the consequences, namely having to wonder whether he/she is self-actualized or self-destructive.

I blame my close-trophobia on the seemingly positive pressure single women face to become "whole." We've been told to indulge ourselves, take baths, take classes, buy houses . . . so we do all that. We're happy with our lives. We're *whole*. But taken to its extreme, "whole" doesn't leave a whole lot of room for anybody else. And I'm not just speaking metaphorically. I'm talking about physical space. For example, I recently reclaimed the center of my bed because I realized sleeping on "my side" implied I was waiting for a guy to fill the other half. Again, good for me, not so good for my future husband. Who I'm not waiting for.

Frankly, I've always maintained that I don't need a man to complete me, but I do need a man to complete the Sunday *New York Times* crossword puzzle. That's the one thing I can't seem to do on my own. So the question for close-trophobes is this: Is it possible to find a mate who fits into our very full lives as nicely as the answers fit into a crossword puzzle, or do we need to learn to leave a little more wiggle room? Skip a spin class for someone. Switch sides of the bed. See what happens when you leave some spaces blank.

chapter thirty-four

RETRODATING: Reconnecting with one of the first boys you ever kissed in order to get back in touch with your own dating innocence and joy.

For the past six months I've been retrodating a guy named Guy.

He was my boyfriend when I was sixteen. We met on a teen tour of Israel. He was from Florida. I was from Oklahoma. We were *In Love*. And we were doomed. Long-distance relationships are tough enough when you're an adult, never mind when you're a kid with no bank account, no frequent flyer miles, and a phone line you share with your parents. We broke up within the year, spent one drunken weekend together in college, then lost touch entirely until his sister saw me on the Golden Globes a couple of years ago and called him. (This, by the way, is why women must always look especially glamorous at awards shows—you never know which ex might be watching.)

I saw Guy last December for the first time in sixteen years. It was love at second sight, and this time around he moved from Florida to be with me, saying he didn't want to lose me again. This would all be wildly romantic if I weren't haunted by the slightly disturbing thought that if he's The One, if I truly knew everything I needed to know about men when I was sixteen, then *what the hell have I been doing for the past twenty years?* What happened to live and learn? What did I pick up, other than emotional baggage? Can it be true that all we really glean from adult relationships is how to be more guarded and overly analytical?

I'd like to believe that's not the case—that we have to go through the heartaches, disappointments, and false starts in order to be clearer about who we are and what we want. (I certainly wouldn't have the same writing career without all this *great* material.) But it's also possible we were better at love when we knew less, and it's time to stop analyzing, stop "growing up" and just enjoy.

That's one of the advantages of retrodating—it brings back your good old naïve, open-hearted self. I can say from experience that kissing the boy you kissed when you were sixteen can make you feel sixteen again, with all the hope and enthusiasm that age implies. This might explain why a surprising number of women I know (seven to be exact) have retrodated, and even married, men they knew as boys. Three of these retrocouples met in the first grade. (They didn't *date* back then, but they did sleep together. At nap time.) And one of those couples—Christine and James—just got engaged. They were each other's first kiss when they were eleven, dated off and on in college, then rediscovered each other as divorcées at their twenty-five-year grammar school reunion. Christine says they both wish they'd been together all along, but hey, better late than never. "You think there's more out there in the world, and then you realize you had it all," she says.

So if you're thinking of missing your reunion because you're not married, bear in mind that you might be missing the retrolove boat. At the very least, spend an afternoon digging through your dusty yearbooks and faded love notes. Even if you don't find an old flame, you might find your old optimistic self. And you might want to give *her* a second chance.

chapter thirty-five

MAN-ME-DOWNS: Men who are passed on from one woman to another after a failed attempt at romance, and the mayhem that inevitably ensues.

Once you're in a decent relationship, it's hard to recall in vivid detail your truly terrible dates. I suspect we forget them much in the same way women forget the pain of childbirth. It's a coping mechanism that helps us continue to propagate the species.

But I did have one terrible date that I do remember, probably because it was not so much terrible for me as it was for him. We were having brunch at an outdoor beach café and a pigeon landed on my date's head, which was laughable . . . the first time. The second time even the other pigeons looked a bit embarrassed for both him and the offending bird. We quickly paid our bill and walked back along the sand at which point he stepped in tar, leading me to remark that it's not often you get tarred and feathered on a first date.

Despite our witty banter and my attraction to him (largely due to his sense of humor in the face of adversity combined with my fear that this mentally challenged pigeon was the sign I'd been waiting for), he eventually made it clear he just wanted to be friends.

I moved on and found the guy I'm currently dating, and Pigeonhead (as I took to calling him) did become a friend, and feeling in love and magnanimous I decided to fix him up with Ellen. Ellen, at this point, was feeling so fed up and demoralized by dating that I was determined to help her have a good experience, even though until recently that wasn't something I could guarantee myself, let alone others. But Ellen is truly beautiful and funny and smart (and very thin) so I figured maybe she would have better luck with Pigeonhead. And she did. They had a great first date, which made me Romance Queen for a Day, and for their second date, Pigeonhead wanted to take her to see Rhett Miller from the band Old 97s. He got four tickets, suggesting we double date, but at the last minute my boyfriend had to leave town so I brought my friend Kate. As we drove home Kate said, "Okay, I have two questions: 1) Why didn't you ever date him? And 2) *How could you not have fixed him up with me?*"

I tried to explain how Ellen was ready to abandon the dating pool forever, whereas Kate had been on approximately three dates in the past week, but she responded that they were all miserable, and Pigeonhead was exactly her type, and he had the best sense of humor, yada yada yada. I knew I could not in good conscience break up a couple I had fixed up. Even having this conversation seemed to violate several rules of dating, not to mention common courtesy. So when Ellen told me weeks later that after many mixed signals Pigeonhead seemed to have deemed her a friend as well, I didn't even mention it to Kate.

I continued *not* to get involved when Pigeonhead started e-mailing Kate, but I had to smile when she called to thank me for my role in her surprisingly delightful Valentine's Day. It was a high degree of difficulty—a first date on the high holy day of romance, but Kate explained that Pigeonhead didn't realize Thursday was Valentine's Day when he proposed the date, and when she pointed it out, he said, "Why not?" I remember as she told me this, I was in a hotel room in New York, and my boyfriend had sent me a beautiful bouquet of flowers, and for the first time in a long time, Kate and I both felt truly optimistic about love.

Kate's next phone call was the announcement that she was completely and officially smitten. I started to think maybe that's why Pigeonhead came into my life—so we could suffer through our date, and Ellen could see Rhett Miller perform live, and Pigeonhead could meet his true love Kate. So you can imagine my surprise when her third phone call—not even an hour later—was the news that Pigeonhead didn't want to date her and she didn't know how many more times she could go through this.

That was it, as far as I was concerned. Three strikes, you're out, baby. It was one thing to reject me. It was another to reject two of my favorite people. So I did something I've never had the nerve to do on my own behalf—I called a guy and asked what the hell he was doing. "YOU CAN'T KEEP TOYING WITH WOMEN'S HEARTS LIKE THIS! IF YOU'RE NOT LOOKING FOR A RELATIONSHIP, YOU HAVE TO STOP DATING! I AM REVOKING YOUR DATING LICENSE!" (I'm not sure I have the power do to this, but that's what I said. Sometimes even once you have a boyfriend you still have a little residual dating anger.)

Pigeonhead sheepishly explained that he *was* looking for a relationship, and he *did* think he might like Kate but when he didn't feel enough of a connection, he didn't want to waste her time or lead her on. As I was yelling "YOU DID LEAD HER ON, YOU LED EVERYBODY ON," I noticed out of the corner of my eye that my Valentine's Day bouquet was still alive, meaning Kate and I had become hysterical over a relationship that didn't have the life span of a flower.

At some point, it seemed, we had become the crazy women men complain about. Of course, no jury of our peers would convict us, because that's what dating does to you after a couple of decades. But still, it was sobering to note that as single women in our thirties, we were as confused and disoriented as that mentally challenged pigeon.

chapter thirty-six

PREMATURE "WE"JACULATION: A common dating dysfunction occurring when one member of a couple starts using the "we" before the other is ready.

First of all, if you are a premature "we"jaculator—do not be embarrassed. You are not alone. (You just aren't encouraged by your love interest to acknowledge that verbally yet.) Premature "we"jaculation is the most common form of dating dysfunction, affecting millions of single women and even an occasional man.

It should be noted that premature "we"jaculation is not a sexual problem, in that it doesn't occur *during* sex. (You rarely hear a woman yell, *"We're* almost there!") But it often occurs as the *result* of sex, since premature sex can lead to premature feelings, which can lead to premature use of the first person plural. Take, for example, the woman who asks, after four dates and a sleepover, "So, how do *we* feel about Japanese food tonight?" or comments to a friend, within earshot of her new beau, *"We've* been so busy, but *we'd* love to get together with you Saturday night!" (Weekends are especially high-risk, since "we" is an essential element of "we"ekend.) Even offhand remarks like these can have a devastating effect on a relationship, as the "we"jaculator receives the message subtly (via dwindling phone calls), or blatantly ("Let's take separate cars to the party") that *we* are not a couple yet.

The problem is most acute when someone (usually a woman who has endured one too many blind dates) is overly eager to become part of a twosome, and someone else (usually a man who has endured one too many "relationship discussions") is reluctant to let go of his single status.

I've personally been on both sides of the "we." I've been accused of premature "we"jaculation after suggesting to a relatively new boyfriend that *we* go on a bike trip at Christmas. This, in his defense, was in April, but by mid-December my "we"phobic friend was still reluctant to commit. He did eventually show, but *we* arrived separately, and *he* required a fully refundable airline ticket and trip insurance. *We* eventually broke up.

I've also experienced the opposite—a guy who was so "we" friendly, he was ready move across the country and live with me after a few great dates. ("C'mon, *we* belong together. *We* should at least give it a shot!") This led to a bit of a freak-out on my part, and made me realize that most of us think we want the "we," but sometimes when we get it too quickly, it's a "we" bit scary. However, *we* (the guy and I) are still together.

Which reminds me, "we"jaculation can continue to cause trouble even after the couple resolves their issues. In fact, once both lovebirds are on board with the "we," things often get worse—not for the couple, but for their single friends. I first noticed this when I was trying to find someone to go with me to *The Sixth Sense*. I was single at the time, and everyone I'd invite would say apologetically, "I promised my boyfriend *we'd* see that together." Or "*We* saw it already." Or "*We* had a feeling the Bruce

Willis character was dead. Oh, wait, sorry—you haven't seen it yet because you're *single*." Okay. Nobody said that. But it was implied.

So be considerate. And remember, the best way to be a *we* is don't lose your *me*.

acknowledgments

For all the dates who made this book possible, thank you for dinner and the stories. Thanks especially to my boyfriends (Jim, Guy, Andy, Scott, Dave, the Lone Ranger whose name I actually forgot, Sam, Brian, Johnie, Steve K., Steve B., Rob from Portland, Benicio, Jonathan, Adam, and Guy again) for always showing up just in time to keep me from becoming cynical.

Thank you to all my friends—especially Kate Adler, Marie Austria, Mark Katz, Heather Maidat, Madeline Wolf, and Joey Xanders—for being there, e-mailing, calling, sharing your tales, and somehow (even when I was heartbroken) making me feel my funniest. Thanks also to the astoundingly talented people I work with who have made commiseration and friendship into an art form—especially Greg Behrendt, Jenny Bicks, Amy B. Harris, Michael Patrick King, John Melfi, Grace Naughton, Julie Rottenberg, Julia Sweeney, Liz Tuccillo, Elisa Zuritsky, and Judy Toll (who was the queen of laughing through adversity, and who we all miss terribly).

A special thanks to Sarah Jessica Parker, Kim Cattrall, Kristin Davis, and Cynthia Nixon for their constant inspiration both on-screen and off-, and to Darren Star for creating a show that is as much fun to write as it is to watch, and which (along with this book) provided me with a much needed creative outlet for my dating anxieties.

Thanks to my lawyers, Gunnar Erickson and Brad Small, who for years ensured that there could be a book even before there was a book; to Cindi Leive, Jill Herzig, and Kristin Van Ogtrop at *Glamour* for seeing me as a "dating expert" and letting me give birth to the Dating Dictionary; and to my assistant Sara Glasser, who read the manuscript in its early stages and gushed so much that I was forced to finish it.

I owe a debt of gratitude to Marty Adelstein and my team at Endeavor (Adriana Alberghetti, Andy Elkin, Ari Emanuel, Brian Lipson, and David Lonner), who despite being in Hollywood were supportive of my decision to spend what is possibly the height of my career working on a little book of essays.

Thanks also to Dan Strone for believing and connecting me with Elizabeth Beier at St. Martin's Press. Elizabeth was a delight from start to finish and probably spoiled me forever. Also, a huge thank you to the amazingly talented artists of Number 17, Emily Oberman and Bonnie Siegler, who brought the book to life with a cover that makes me happy every time I look at it.

Thanks, finally, to my teacher, Virginia Davis, who convinced me in the third grade that I was a writer; to Betsy Carter, who published my first humorous essay ("The *Real* New York Marathon") in a magazine she founded; to Wendy Goldman, who saw the essay and told me to think about sitcom writing; and to my parents, who read, watched, and saved everything I ever wrote.